D0332184

Improving Leadership
Performance

IMPROVING LEADERSHIP PERFORMANCE

Peter L. Wright and David S. Taylor
University of Bradford Management Centre

Prentice/Hall International

Englewood Cliffs, NJ   London   New Delhi   Rio de Janeiro
Singapore   Sydney   Tokyo   Toronto   Wellington

Library of Congress Cataloging in Publication Data
Wright, Peter L.
  Improving leadership performance.

  Includes bibliographical references and index.
    1. Leadership. I. Taylor, David S., 1940-
II. Title.
HD57.7.W75   1984   658.4'092   84-8226

ISBN 0-13-452673-2

British Library Cataloging in Publication Data
Wright, Peter L.
  Improving leadership performance.
    1. Management   2. Leadership
  I. Title   II. Taylor, David S.
  658.4'092   HD38

ISBN 0-13-452673-2

ISBN 0-13-452673 2

Prentice-Hall International, Inc., London
Prentice-Hall of Australia Pty, Ltd, Sydney
Prentice-Hall Canada, Inc, Toronto
Prentice-Hall of India Private, Ltd, New Delhi
Prentice-Hall of Japan, Inc, Tokyo
Prentice-Hall of Southeast Asia Pte, Ltd, Singapore
Prentice-Hall Inc, Englewood Cliffs, New Jersey
Prentice-Hall do Brasil Ltda, Rio de Janeiro
Whitehall Books Ltd, Wellington, New Zealand

Typeset in England by Typesetters (Birmingham) Ltd
Printed in the United States of America

10 9 8 7 6 5 4 3 2 1

To Barbara and Marian

Contents

Preface

This book represents a new departure in the study of leadership. We believe that leadership is like most other human activities. The skilful person tends to perform better than an unskilful one. Yet the concept of skill is virtually unused in leadership theory. Early theorists took the view that it was the individual's personality which determined the degree of leadership success. When relatively little progress was made with this approach, theorists turned to the idea that it was what leaders did—their leadership style—rather than what they were, which determined their success. Thus we now have a vast and confusing vocabulary of terms describing the way leaders behave, such as autocratic, democratic, authoritarian, employee-oriented, person-oriented, task-oriented, to mention only a few of the more common ones. However, the question of leadership skill is rarely, if ever, mentioned. Theorists are very concerned with *what* style or approach leaders should apply in different situations, but not with *how well* they apply them. This we believe is one of the major limitations of modern leadership theory. In this book we have attempted to overcome this limitation by describing both a framework for the analysis of the interpersonal skills of leadership and methods for their training and development.

Our aim is to help managers to develop the interpersonal skills needed to fulfil their leadership role effectively. We have no desire to develop a grand theory of leadership. To use an analogy, we would regard ourselves as tool developers rather than theory builders. We would rather supply managers with a set of behavioural tools from which they can select the one most appropriate to handle a particular leadership situation, than develop a grand theory which explains everything but has few real practical implications. Unfortunately, much of modern leadership theory seems to fall into the latter category.

We have taken a different approach to the study of leadership partly because our original interest was interpersonal skills training rather than leadership itself. Our interest in leadership grew out of what has come to be known as the 'Bradford Approach' to interviewing training. This was initially developed by Gerry Randell and his colleagues in the context of performance appraisal interviews.* However, it was later extended by ourselves and others into such areas as grievance, disciplinary and audit interviewing.§

The more we extended this work, the more it appeared to us that our basic approach—regarding the effective handling of relationships between people in terms of precisely defined interpersonal skills—was not limited to any one particular type of interaction. That is, although we were ostensibly training people to carry out a particular kind of interview, we were in fact training people in skills which had much wider managerial applications. In particular, it seemed we were training people in skills which would be useful in virtually any interaction between manager and subordinates. Rather to our surprise, therefore, we came to the conclusion that, implicitly, we were training people in leadership skills.

We were aware, of course, that interpersonal skills training had been successfully applied in such areas as counselling, encounter groups and mental health,° and developments in such areas had been a major source of influence in our approach to managerial problems. Indeed, we have occasionally received informal feedback from our course members that the training had also had beneficial effects on their personal and social lives. Nevertheless, there was, as far as we know, neither a fully developed practical nor theoretical framework for the application of an interpersonal skills approach to leadership theory and training. This book is our attempt to develop such a framework.

One other consequence of arriving at the study of leadership through interpersonal skills training is a belief in learning through practice with feedback and guidance. Simply reading a book may provide knowledge, but actual performance is unlikely to improve to any great extent until the reader has tried something out in practice, received feedback on what has been achieved and guidance on how to do better next time. In training in interpersonal skills, we have typically used interview role plays for this purpose. Obviously we cannot do this for individual readers. What we have done, however, is to include exercises which will enable readers to practise many of the skills discussed and check their answers against the 'model' answers in the appendices. In the final section of the book, we also describe both a formal training course in interpersonal skills and a number of ways in which individual readers can practise their interpersonal skills and obtain feedback and guidance for themselves.

*GA Randell, PMA Packard, RL Shaw and AJ Slater (1972), *Staff Appraisal*, Institute of Personnel Management.
§RWT Gill and DS Taylor (1976), 'Training Managers to Handle Discipline and Grievance Interviews', *Journal of European Training*, Vol. 5, pp. 217–227.
DS Taylor and PL Wright (1977), 'Training Auditors in Interviewing Skills', *Journal of European Industrial Training*, Vol. 1, pp. 8–16.
°See for example, G Egan (1975), *The Skilled Helper: A Model for Systematic Helping and Interpersonal Relating*. Monterey, Ca, Brooks/Cole; G Egan (1976), *Interpersonal Living: A Skills/Contract Approach to Human Relations Training in Groups*, Monterey, Ca, Brooks/Cole; P Trower, B Bryant and M Argyle (1978), *Social Skills and Mental Health*, Methuen.

Improving Leadership Performance

Chapter 1

A Skills Approach to Leadership

INTRODUCTION

The practice of leadership is concerned with influencing peoples' behaviour and feelings. Consider some examples:

An army sergeant yells, what to an outsider would be an unintelligible command, and a squad of thirty soldiers come simultaneously to attention, standing stiffly and impassively.

A Sales Director listens to one of her Brand Managers outline his plan for combatting a competitor's newly introduced product. She merely nods and says 'uh huh' occasionally and when he has finished says, 'Yes, that seems like a good way of tackling the problem. Why don't you go ahead and implement it.' The Brand Manager leaves smiling and walks purposefully back to his own office.

A Production Foreman says to a sheet metal worker, 'For the last time Joe, when you use that machine, you must have the safety guard in place. If I see you using it without the guard again, I'm going to institute formal disciplinary proceedings against you.' The worker looks resentful, but complies.

The Departmental Manager looks around his group and says 'Now this is an important decision, and as you know I don't believe in autocratic management, so I want the decision to arise out of a free and frank discussion among the group. His subordinates look bored and resigned. "Here we go," one mutters, "we will spend all afternoon being manipulated into accepting the solution he came in with in the first place. Why doesn't he simply tell us. At least an autocrat doesn't waste your time with tedious discussions".'

"You will do it my way or else", bellows the irate Section Leader. "In that case, you can keep your job. I quit!" yells back the Research Chemist, throws her lab coat in the corner of the room and stalks out of the lab, slamming the door behind her.

In each of these examples, someone is trying to influence the behaviour of another individual or group. These attempts at influence tend to have emotional consequences for the people concerned. They may feel enthusiastic about the task in question or be so resentful that they refuse to do it, or do it badly. They may regard the person attempting to influence them with admiration and respect, amusement and disdain, or fear and dislike. They may believe that their role within the leader's group is worthwhile and meaningful or feel so dissatisfied with it that they would leave at the first reasonable opportunity. Such beliefs and feelings are extremely important to the leader, whether he or she knows it or not. In varying degrees, they will determine not only the success of the leader's immediate attempt at influence, but also the probability of being able to influence the same individual successfully in future.

To summarize, we regard leadership as an activity, that of influencing the behaviour, beliefs and feelings of other group members in an intended direction. However, we shall not be concerned with all forms of influence or even all forms of leadership in this book. For example, influence may take place at a distance without any personal interaction between the people concerned. The marketing executive who plans an advertising campaign wishes to influence the attitudes and buying behaviour of potential customers. Similarly, the politician planning a political campaign wishes to influence the attitudes and voting behaviour of the electorate, most of whom he or she will not meet personally. On the other hand, each of these people is likely to have a group of subordinates or staff with whom he or she interacts on a more personal basis. It is with leadership in such situations, where influence takes place within a relatively small group allowing personal contact, that the present book is primarily concerned.

Furthermore, although much of what we say will have relevance to leadership in informal groups, our main emphasis will be on leadership in formal organizations. That is, we are primarily concerned with situations where people are appointed or elected to leadership positions and are expected by the organization to be the major source of influence on the work behaviour of a particular group or organization members. For the sake of convenience, we shall refer to the parties involved as manager and subordinate(s).

Whilst our main concern is with hierarchical leadership, there are, of course, other relationships in which the ability to influence work behaviour is important. At times managers may need to influence their fellow managers and even their own superiors in order to achieve their performance objectives. Many of the skills we discuss will also be relevant in such situations.

We realize that defining leadership solely in terms of influence can give rise to an apparent anomaly. If a successful leader is one who has considerable influence on the follower's behaviour, then a leader who makes the wrong decision and leads a group into disaster is a more successful leader than one who fails to influence the group and thereby avoids disaster.[1] However, we take the view that leadership is only one part of a manager's job.[2] To expand the concept of leadership to include decision-making skill, technical expertise, and all the other attributes necessary to succeed as a manager, would not be helpful. It would make the concept of leadership far too broad. Specifying what it is that enables a leader to influence follower behaviour is difficult enough, without having simultaneously to take into account other major facets of managerial performance. Furthermore, expanding the concept of leadership in this way, would render it synonymous with management, and make the term virtually redundant. We shall therefore be concentrating on one aspect of a manager's job, that of influencing subordinate behaviour and feelings, and this activity we shall call leadership.

The aim of this book is to enable managers to perform their leadership role more successfully by improving their ability to influence the work performance of their subordinates, and their feelings about their work. We would argue that one of the key factors in successful leadership, and certainly the one most readily improved, is the possession of certain specific interpersonal skills on the part of the manager. This emphasis on skills, rather than the leader's personality, attitude, style and so on, inevitably has implications for leadership training. We believe that successful leadership behaviour can be learned, and that the most effective way of learning it is by the acquisition of the relevant interpersonal skills through practice with feedback and guidance.

CURRENT APPROACHES TO LEADERSHIP THEORY

Most current theories of leadership are behavioural in the sense that they are concerned with the behaviours, rather than personality traits, which are presumed to be associated with effective leadership. Nevertheless, such behaviours tend to be described at a relatively high level of abstraction. This is particularly true of leadership style theories, where terms such as consideration, concern for production, employee-centred, participative, task-oriented and democratic, abound. These concepts describe very broad classes of behaviour, but the behaviours themselves are rarely discussed in any detail. It seems to be assumed that actual and potential leaders are fully aware of the complete range of behaviours which exist under any one heading, and what is more can perform them perfectly if need be.

The inherent vagueness of the style approach was recognized by Vroom and Yetton[3] in their normative model of leadership. They advanced instead a number of different decision-making methods which the leader could employ, such as obtaining the necessary information from subordinates, sharing the problem with subordinates, delegating the problem to a subordinate, and so on. This undoubtedly comes closer to describing actual leader behaviour than the leadership styles approach, but Vroom and Yetton still do not tell leaders how they should go about obtaining information and sharing or delegating problems, let alone how to go about it skilfully. Again, it seems to be assumed that leaders will somehow know this intuitively and simply need to be guided to the right general approach to the problem.

Fiedler[4] apparently avoids this problem by arguing that one should not attempt to modify leader behaviour (because this is too difficult) but should modify the leader's situation instead. However, when one examines the methods which he suggests leaders should use to change their situation one finds that they include such *behaviours* as "organizing some off-work group activities which include your subordinates (e.g. picnics, boating, softball teams, excursion)", or "trying to be one of the gang by playing down any trappings of power or rank." As in other situational theories, such behaviours are merely given as a few examples of the *kind* of thing the leader might do. No attempt is made to provide a comprehensive account of the behaviours concerned nor is there any discussion of the skills required to perform them well. One doubts, for example, whether subordinates invited to play softball by a disliked, socially inept superior would necessarily find this a rewarding experience.

Recently, however, a number of researchers have been studying the effect of more specific aspects of the leader's behaviour on subordinates' work performance and attitudes.[5] These more specific behaviours include rewarding good performance (e.g. giving recognition and merit increases), punishing poor performance (e.g. giving reprimands or stopping pay increases), setting goals, providing feedback, redesigning jobs to provide greater personal fulfilment, and so on. In general, such studies show that these managerial activities do have a marked beneficial effect on subordinates' work performance. The one exception is punishment which appears to have little effect, or even a negative one.

Encouraging as this work is, it does not go far enough in our opinion. It does not take into account the crucial question of how *skilfully* the managers perform the behaviours in question. For example, praise done well can have beneficial effects, but done badly can equally give rise to adverse reactions, such as embarrassment, resentment and loss of respect. Thus, the practical implications of these studies are less apparent than they seem at first sight. An obvious conclusion would seem to be that managers should avoid punishing poor performance and concentrate upon rewarding good performance. However, as there is little advice on how to do this skilfully, it is distinctly possible that the erstwhile punitive manager, taking this lesson to heart, will turn into an ineffectual 'nice guy', embarrassing to and distrusted by his subordinates. Furthermore, we are left with a lingering doubt concerning the negative relationships found between punitive behaviour and subordinate performance in these studies. Punishment is also something which can be done more or less well. Often it seems to be done badly, perhaps because the behaviour usually represents an emotional response on the part of the punisher rather than a skilful attempt to influence subsequent behaviour. Thus there is the possibility that all these results show is that *unskilful* punitive behaviour has negative effects on performance.[6]

In addition the studies do not take into account individual differences between subordinates. Some may resent criticism more than others, some may respond well to praise whilst others tend to find it embarrassing, some might be motivated by a more challenging job whilst others may prefer more routine work. Thus general solutions are likely to be less effective than those designed to suit the needs of specific subordinates. Recognizing the individual needs of subordinates and modifying accordingly the way they are treated is also something which requires considerable skill on the part of the manager.

In summary, then, we would argue that there are two major gaps in current approaches to the study of leadership. Firstly, there is insufficient emphasis on what leaders actually do when they interact with their followers. Secondly, the element of skill is largely ignored. Even when researchers do examine more specific leadership behaviours, they do not consider how well, or how badly, the leaders perform the behaviours in question. This book represents an attempt to overcome these limitations by describing a taxonomy of leadership behaviour which can be used as a framework for the analysis and development of leadership skills.

A SKILLS APPROACH TO LEADERSHIP

We would suggest that the manager's behaviour in interactions with his or her subordinates can be examined in terms of three different levels of analysis.

1. Primary Components Here we are concerned with what managers actually say and do—their verbal and nonverbal behaviour—in interactions with their subordinates. Verbal behaviour includes the manager's use of questions and statements to gather information from subordinates, influence their work behaviour, handle grievances, and so on. Nonverbal behaviour consists of the tones of voice, gestures, body postures, facial expressions which accompany speech, often changing its meaning in significant ways, and sometimes even replacing it altogether.

2. Structural Factors This refers to the way in which the primary components are sequenced, or in longer interactions to the way in which the interaction as a whole or topics covered within it are introduced, sequenced, resolved, linked together, and so on.

3. The Overall Approach The components used in an interaction and the way it is structured will depend at least in part upon the type of interaction the manager wishes to have with a subordinate. Two main factors are important here. One is the extent to which the manager is prepared to allow the subordinate to influence the content of the interaction and the decisions which are reached. The other is the extent to which the manager wishes to conduct the interaction in a warm, friendly manner or one which is cold and businesslike, emphasizing differences in status. It is at this level of analysis that our approach most resembles that of traditional leadership theorists. However, there are important differences as we shall see later.

We would regard the interpersonally skilled leader as one who:

- has a wide variety of verbal components (question and statement types) at his or her disposal and is able to select the one most appropriate for the situation and particular purpose at hand, and perform it well, with the appropriate nonverbal cues;

- can structure interactions effectively by organizing these questions and statements into purposeful sequences which impel the interaction towards its objective(s);
- can develop an approach to the interaction, which is appropriate to the objectives in question and the probable reactions of the subordinate.

Our analysis of the behavioural skills of leadership forms the central core of this book. Verbal and nonverbal components are discussed in Chapters 4 and 5 respectively, structural factors in Chapter 6 and approaches to manager – subordinate interactions in Chapter 7.

In addition to behavioural skills, however, two other types of skill are required for the successful management of people at work. Firstly, there are the diagnostic skills which are required to identify what needs to be done to maintain high levels of work performance, and to improve it where necessary. To achieve this, the manager must have a good understanding of the range of factors which affect performance, such as motivation, abilities, feedback, and so on. Furthermore, the manager must know what actions can be taken to influence these various factors, and through them performance itself. This question will be examined in Chapter 2.

Secondly, the successful management of people requires accurate perception and evaluation of people and events. This is important in the analysis of work performance, e.g. establishing what are the major factors influencing a subordinate's work performance and whether there are areas in which improvement is desirable. It is also important in interactions with subordinates where sensitivity to the other person's responses can enable the manager to pick up low level cues concerning his or her beliefs, feelings and intentions which might otherwise have been missed. The perceptual skills of leadership are discussed in Chapter 3.

Finally, in Chapter 8 we examine ways in which the interpersonal skills of leadership can be acquired and developed, both in formal training courses and by the individual manager working on his or her own.

ETHICAL CONSIDERATIONS

One subject which is rarely, if ever, discussed in books on leadership is the ethics of helping one person to exert greater influence over another. Early leadership style theorists neatly avoided the problem by claiming that showing consideration or concern for people was the most effective way of increasing subordinates' productivity. Thus there was no conflict for the manager being trained, who could be organizationally effective and a 'nice guy' at the same time. Even the later situational theorists avoided the problem to a large degree, by defining so vaguely their leadership styles and the expected consequences of using them, that one did not feel that real people were involved in the process. We, on the other hand, are concerned with much more specific leader behaviours aimed at producing specific subordinate responses. Thus the question inevitably arises: "Who is to benefit from any increase in the manager's influence over his or her subordinates?" Are we, for example, preaching manipulation? As scientists, we can avoid these problems by claiming that we are concerned only with what objectively does happen as a result of actions taken, not with what should happen. As trainers, however, we *are* concerned with the effects on other people of the training we give: the ethical implications are important.

It seems to be a requirement of any organization that certain people are made responsible for the performance of others. How the role is distributed, whether it is unitary, shared or alternated, the way in which it is performed, will depend upon the philosophy and culture of the organization. Nevertheless, where individuals are responsible for the performance of others, influence is inevitably involved. One cannot be held responsible for the performance of people over whom one has no influence.

However, this should not imply that the influence is necessarily authoritarian. Even the most democratic forms of management need someone to be responsible for sounding out member's opinions, organizing voting, ensuring that everyone has an opportunity to express their views, and so on. If, however, the democratic leader fails through lack of skill to influence his or her followers to behave democratically, then the democratic process itself may fail.

Similarly, skilful influence does not necessarily imply manipulation. If the leader skilfully influences a follower to do something for the leader's benefit without the follower realizing it, then manipulation is involved. On the other hand, if the leader influences a follower to do something for the follower's benefit, with the follower's knowledge and consent, then one would refer to the activity by a much kinder name, such as career development, job enrichment, and so on.

Much the same skills are involved in behaviour influence whatever the motives of the manager concerned. Thus, providing leadership training does increase the danger that such skills may be used for selfish purposes. On the other hand, failure to provide such training may also prevent genuinely concerned managers from effectively helping or developing their subordinates. Our response to this dilemma is to regard training in interpersonal skills as the lesser risk. Being managed by someone with an autocratic style but little real influence can be much worse than being managed by a skilful autocratic. Similarly, the skilful democrat may be a more pleasant boss to work for, but the chaos which ensues under an ineffective one can drive subordinates to despair. Whilst each subordinate may enjoy his or her own freedom of action caused by a boss with low influence, the unfortunate fact remains that all the boss's other subordinates will have equal freedom of action. Thus obtaining their cooperation, when interests conflict, can be a time-consuming and emotionally exhausting business. It is at times like these when one sometimes hears a heartfelt plea for a dictator to make a decision either way. Our view is that a more appropriate plea would be for a skilful manager with greater ability to influence subordinates. An authoritarian decision might be an appropriate way to solve the problem, but equally, a skilful democrat might influence the individuals concerned to solve the problem in a participative way to their mutual satisfaction.

Thus, in the final analysis, it comes down to a choice between being managed skilfully or managed unskilfully. Our own feeling, supported by the research evidence, is that people prefer working for interpersonally skilful managers. It is the ineffective manager who is disliked most, irrespective of his or her managerial style or motives.[7]

NOTES AND REFERENCES

1 D Katz and RL Kahn (1978), *The Social Psychology of Organizations*, 2nd edn., John Wiley.

2 H Mintzberg (1975), 'The Manager's Job: Folklore and Fact', *Harvard Business Review*, Vol. 53, July/Aug., pp.49–61.

3 VH Vroom and PW Yetton (1973), *Leadership and Decision Making*, University of Pittsburgh Press.

4 FE Fiedler, MM Chambers and L Mahar (1976), *Improving Leadership Effectiveness: The Leadermatch Concept*, John Wiley.

5 HP Sims (1977), 'The Leader as Manager of Reinforcement Contingencies: An Empirical Example and a Model', in JG Hunt and LL Larson, (eds), *Leadership: The Cutting Edge*, Southern Illinois University Press.
   AD Szilagyi (1980), 'Causal Inferences Between Leader Reward Behaviour and Subordinate Performance, Absenteeism and Work Satisfaction', *Journal of Occupational Psychology*, Vol. 53, pp.195–204.
   GR Oldham (1976), 'The Motivational Strategies Used by Supervisors: Relationships to Effectiveness Indicators', *Organisational Behaviour and Human Performance*, Vol. 15, pp.66–86.
   GA Yukl and L Kanuk (1979), 'Leadership Behaviour and Effectiveness of Beauty Salon Managers', *Personnel Psychology*, Vol. 32, pp.663–675.

6 Some support for this notion can be found in research on attitude change. Early research appeared to show that high fear arousal was less likely to produce changes in behaviour than moderate or low levels of fear arousal (IL Janis and S Feshback (1953), 'Effects of Fear-arousing Communications', *Journal of Abnormal and Social Psychology*, Vol. 48, pp.78–92.) However, later research showed that high fear arousal could be more effective than low fear arousal in producing attitude change providing the subject was provided with an effective plan of action to avoid the fear arousing situation (H Levinthal, R Singer and S Jones (1965), Effects of Fear and Specificity of Recommendation Upon Attitudes and Behaviour', *Journal of Personality and Social Psychology*, Vol. 2, pp.20–29).

7 PJ Sadler (1970), 'Leadership Style, Confidence in Management, and Job Satisfaction', *Journal of Applied Behavioural Science*, Vol. 6, pp.3–19.

Chapter 2

The Diagnostic Skills of Leadership

Geoff's Performance

Geoff, a 20 year old draughtsman, works in an architects office. He has been with this firm for three years during which time he has been accountable to four different architects, each of whom gave him drawings to do. The four architects have felt for some time that Geoff has been working at an unacceptable level. However, when any of the four have questionned him about his work, he has played one off against another. One architect recently left and a new one has just been appointed. It has been decided to channel all work for Geoff through the newly appointed architect Clive, so that he can monitor the work.

From casual observation and interaction, Clive has noticed that Geoff spends a significant amount of time in personal activities such as talking to the girls in the typing pool, talking to friends on the telephone and going for frequent drinks from the coffee machine.

His main work involves making drawings and plans for buildings, from specifications and sketches produced by the four architects. Other tasks include filing these, after photocopying, maintaining his own equipment, ordering supplies of paper, pencils, pens and ink etc. Throughout Clive's period of observation and interaction there has been a backlog of work causing frustration and anger to the architects. Further, some of the drawings have had to be returned by the architects, because they have not been to specification, contain drawing errors and/or omissions.

One of the architects has no doubt about the cause of the problem, or what should be done about it. "He is bone idle and bloody minded", the architect said to Clive, "he should be told that he either performs up to standard or he will be sacked." However, Clive wonders whether there might be other explanations for Geoff's poor performance and other ways of dealing with it.

Before reading this chapter, list what reasons you think there might be for Geoff's below-standard performance and the steps which might be taken to improve it. Treat these as hypotheses to be checked out later. Do not worry if some of them are contradictory.

INTRODUCTION

All organizations face the problem of how to influence their members to work effectively towards the achievement of organizational objectives. One way of tackling this problem is through the institution and improvement of organizational systems. Examples include financial control systems, management information systems, personnel appraisal and development systems, industrial relations systems, and so on. Alternatively, one can tackle the problem on an individual basis and attempt to discover just what it is that would help each employee to become more effective at his or her own job.

Of course, one can attempt to improve both organizational systems and individual performance at the same time. Our impression, however, is that organizations, or rather those people who run them, are usually more concerned with getting the systems right. This is understandable. If an organizational systems fails, this can have immediate adverse effects on the whole organization. It may run out of money or there may be a prolonged strike. If an individual performs badly in his or her job, this will embarrass the immediate superior and inconvenience colleagues and customers or clients, but in most cases it will not be a disaster in organizational terms. Furthermore, improving the performance of all the members of an organization on an individual basis seems like an extremely daunting task. Redesigning or tightening up organizational systems is apparently much easier. It can also be seen to be done and thus receive credit, whereas handling a subordinate well is much less visible and more likely to be overlooked. However, we would argue that it is a mistake to ignore the individual. People have a marvellous ability to sabotage even the most carefully designed systems. One finds financial control systems which encourage unnecessary spending because money not spent before the end of the financial year is lost; complex management information systems which contain misleading data because the managers who supply it find it too much trouble, or too incriminating, to give accurate information; personnel appraisal systems with impressive forms to which managers merely pay lip service and write "Same as last year", and so on. One of the standard jokes in personnel appraisal circles concerns the personnel manager who checked back through years of forms each of which said "Same as last year" about a particular employee, until he found the first form which said "Too soon to tell"!

Furthermore, whilst the performance of a single individual might not make much difference in organizational terms, the summated performance of all the individuals in an organization will have a major impact on organizational effectiveness. Think what a difference it would make if each individual in an organization improved his or her performance by even a moderate amount!

Achieving this improvement in performance and maintaining existing high levels of performance is an important part of the manager's leadership role. Organizational life would often be chaotic without systems, but no matter how well designed the systems, they cannot work on their own. They have to be

Ability and motivation are undoubtedly key factors in work performance. An individual will not perform well at a task unless he or she *wants* to perform well and has the necessary *ability* to turn this desire into actual high performance.

Supposing then, that a manager feels that performance is below standard in some area, or even if adequate could be improved even further. What should the manager do? Sooner or later, it will be necessary to talk to the individual(s) concerned. It may be to tell them what to do differently, ask them what is going wrong, or influence their behaviour in more subtle and indirect ways. The more skilfully these interactions are handled, the more likely the manager will achieve the desired performance improvement. These interactive skills will be discussed in later chapters.

ANALYZING WORK PERFORMANCE

There is more to effective leadership influence than simply interacting skilfully with subordinates. Skills of analysis are also required. To take *relevant* steps to improve performance, a manager must be able to pinpoint precisely what the performance problem is, and identify both the reasons for the problem and the steps which can be taken to solve it. In dealing with the complexities of human behaviour "the successful manager must be a good diagnostician and value a spirit of inquiry".[1] Because of the complexity of human beings and their work roles, the reasons for, and most appropriate solutions to, performance problems vary from person to person and from job to job. Thus managers who make narrow and stereotyped assumptions about the nature of performance problems, whether it is that poor performers are "bone idle and bloody minded", or that they merely need the right opportunity to release their natural energy and creativity, can only be right some of the time. Inevitably they will also be wrong in the remaining cases and as a result select less appropriate solutions or worse, inappropriate ones.

Unfortunately, although leadership and motivation theorists have now largely accepted the complexity of human behaviour, they have done remarkably little to help managers develop the improved diagnostic skills required. They have certainly described the complexities quite well, but that is not enough. What is also required are training techniques and diagnostic tools which will help managers to improve their diagnosis of performance. Much less work has been done in this area.

To improve diagnostic skills, we would suggest that the first requirement is an understanding of the *range* of factors which can influence job performance. Early writers on work performance tended to assume that it was influenced by a relatively small number of factors. A much quoted formula put forward during the 1950s, for example, attempted to account for differences in performance levels in terms of only two variables:[2]

Performance = Ability × Motivation

managed all the way down the line. Furthermore, even without a supporting system there is a great deal which the individual manager can do to improve the performance of each subordinate for which he or she is responsible.

Important as they are, however, ability and motivation are not the only factors influencing levels of work performance. The obvious omission is resources. Even a highly motivated, skilful surgeon is unlikely to perform a high quality operation armed only with a rusty penknife. When analyzing performance problems with students and managers, therefore, we modified the formula to read:

Performance $= F$ (Ability $\times$ Motivation $\times$ Resources)

This proved to be only a slight improvement. We still received many suggested reasons for, or solutions to, performance problems which could not readily be attributed to any of these three factors.

At about the same time, dissatisfaction with the simplicity of early attempts to explain work performance also became apparent in the literature, and more and more complex formulae began to appear. One, for example, suggested that:[3]

Performance $= F$ (aptitude level $\times$ skill level $\times$ understanding of the task $\times$ choice to expend effort $\times$ choice of degree of effort to expend $\times$ choice to persist $\times$ facilitating and inhibiting conditions not under the control of the individual)

This may provide a more comprehensive description of the factors influencing performance but it is far from ideal as a diagnostic tool. Its apparent complexity would tend to discourage managers and students from using it. Furthermore, it does not give any indication of the actions which might be taken to solve the performance problem once the reasons for it have been identified. Finally, the pseudo-mathematical nature of such formulae can also be a drawback. The variables included almost certainly do influence performance in some way, but they are extremely difficult to measure and the precise relationships between them are unknown. In reality, therefore, these formulae represent no more than a convenient way of listing a number of relevant variables. To scientifically trained managers and students, however, it can appear that they represent an example of psychologists overclaiming the scientific rigour of their subject and further reduce their acceptability.

For all these reasons, therefore, we decided to look for an alternative method of analyzing performance problems. One approach which appeared much more promising was to use a flowchart, as do Mager and Pipe.[4] However, this flowchart did not include a number of factors which we felt had an important influence on performance. We attempted to incorporate these into an expanded flowchart, but this turned out to be too large and complex to be practical. We therefore decided that a checklist, which could be set out quite easily on one side of a sheet of paper, would be both easier to follow and to use in practical situations. The checklist that we developed is shown in Figure 1.

FIGURE 1 Checklist for Improving Work Performance

1 What is the problem in behavioural terms? What precisely is the individual doing or not doing which is adversely influencing his or her performance?
2 Is the problem **really** serious enough to spend time and effort on?
3 What reasons might there be for the performance problem? (See colomn 1)
4 What actions might be taken to improve the situation? (See column 2)

Possible Reasons For Performance Problem	Possible Solutions
Goal clarity Is the person fully aware of the job requirements?	Give guidance concerning expected goals and standards. Set targets. MBO.
Ability Does the person have the capacity to do the job well?	Provide formal training, on the job coaching, practice, secondment, etc.
Task difficulty Does the person find the task too demanding?	Simplify task, reduce work load, reduce time pressures, etc.
Intrinsic motivation Does the person find the task rewarding in itself?	Redesign job to match job-holder's needs
Extrinsic motivation Is good perform-ance rewarded by others?	Arrange positive consequences for good performance and zero or negative consequences for poor performance
Feedback Does the person receive adequate feedback about his/her performance?	Provide or arrange feedback
Resources Does the person have adequate resources for satisfactory task performance?	Provide staff, equipment, raw materials as appropriate
Working conditions Do working conditions, physical or social, inter-fere with performance?	Improve light, noise, heat, layout, remove distractions, etc. as appro-priate

5 Do you have sufficient information to select the most appropriate solution(s)? If not, collect the information required, e.g. consult records, observe work behaviour, talk to person concerned
6 Select most appropriate solution(s)
7 Is the solution worthwhile in cost–benefit terms?
 (a) If so, implement it
 (b) If not, work through the checklist again, or relocate the individual, **or** reorganize the department/organization, **or** live with the problem
8 Could you have handled the problem better? If so, review own performance. If not, and the problem is solved, reward yourself and tackle next problem.

A CHECKLIST FOR IMPROVING WORK PERFORMANCE

What is the Problem?

The checklist suggests that if a manager believes that he or she has a performance problem, the first thing to do is to define the problem in terms of behaviour. What precisely is the individual doing or not doing which is adversely affecting his or her performance?

In our experience of both the comments put on performance appraisal forms and the statements made on appraisal interviewing courses, managers typically describe performance problems in terms of vague, and usually derogatory personality defects. For example, the problem arises because the individual lacks self confidence, lacks initiative, is indiscreet, or is too aggressive. This renders the problem virtually unsolvable. Many managers take the view that the adult personality is virtually fixed and certainly outside their skill to change. Consequently, they regard attempts to improve performance as a waste of time. There is much to be said for this view. Telling individuals that they possess a personality defect and should rectify it *is* a waste of time. Most people would strongly resent it, and even if they did accept the 'advice', it is extremely unlikely that they would know how to go about changing their personality in the suggested direction.

On the other hand, these individuals must have done something to lead the manager to believe that they have personality defects, such as, say, lacking initiative. Perhaps an individual sits around waiting to be told what to do after finishing one task instead of finding another one to do; or does not order supplies sufficiently far ahead for them to be available when needed; or does not contribute to departmental meetings, only speaking when spoken to, and so on. These are much more manageable problems. They are examples of behaviours which people can modify, if approached in the right way.

Furthermore, defining the problem in behavioural terms avoids an ethical problem for the manager. Asking employees to change their personalities could be regarded as an unacceptable invasion of personal privacy. Asking employees to change their work behaviour is a legitimate part of the manager's job. Influencing work behaviour is largely what managers are paid for.

How Serious is the Problem?

Secondly, the checklist suggests that the manager should consider very carefully whether the problem is really serious enough to merit the time and effort which will have to be spent putting it right. This is put in to encourage managers to examine whether the behaviour is really having a serious effect on the individual's work performance or simply offends the manager's prejudices about particular types of people, styles of dress, ways of doing a job, and so on.

Assuming that the problem is serious enough to merit expenditure of time and effort, the checklist next suggests that the manager should attempt to discover the reason or reasons for the problem. Of course, the job-holders themselves are likely to be a rich source of information concerning the possible causes of their performance problems (and also the steps which might be taken to improve the situation). Thus a discussion with the job-holders to obtain their views will almost invariably be necessary. Before this, however, we would suggest that managers review the situation in order to get their thoughts in order for the subsequent discussion.

Why has it Occurred?

Eight basic reasons for inadequate work performance are listed.

(i) Goal Clarity
The employee may either not know that a particular part of a job is important or be unaware of the standard of performance expected in a particular area. The latter can also include the situation in which an employee is working to too high a standard and perhaps thereby producing items too slowly.

(ii) Ability
The individual may lack the skills or knowledge necessary for satisfactory task performance.

(iii) Task Difficulty
In some circumstances, it may be more appropriate to regard the task as being too difficult for the job-holder, rather than attributing poor performance to the individual's lack of ability. For example, the job may be more complex, involve more different aspects, or entail shorter deadlines than the individual can cope with.

(iv) Intrinsic Motivation
The employee may not find the job rewarding in itself. That is, it does not provide the interest, challenge, opportunities for achievement, etc. which the individual would like to experience.

(v) Extrinsic Motivation
Perhaps the individual believes that good performance will not be rewarded, or may even be punished, by other people, e.g. his or her boss, colleagues, customers, etc. Extrinsic rewards include such things as salary, promotion, recognition, social acceptance, and so on.

(vi) Feedback
Poor performance at work may continue because the employee does not receive any feedback indicating that performance is below standard, or lacks crucial information which would indicate in what way performance should be modified in order to improve it.

(vii) Resources
The individual may lack the necessary human or physical resources to perform the task adequately, e.g. equipment, raw materials, support services, etc.

(viii) Working Conditions
A variety of factors in the individual's working environment can impair levels of work performance. These include: (a) *physical environment*, e.g. illumination, noise, atmospheric conditions (odour, heat, humidity); (b) *social environment*, e.g. relations with supervisors or colleagues; and (c) *conditions of service*, e.g. hours of work, rest periods, work schedules, etc. Inadequate conditions in any of these areas can give rise to reduced concentration, health and safety hazards, morale problems, labour turnover, strikes and so on.[5]

The above eight factors we regard as the basic influences on work performance. It would be possible to generate more by subdividing them further or by describing the circumstances which cause these problems to arise. For example, lack of ability has been subdivided into lack of skill and lack of aptitude.[6] Similarly, it would be possible to introduce factors such as 'difficult domestic circumstances' or 'poor relations with colleagues', which might reveal themselves as 'lack of motivation' or 'lack of resources' respectively. However, the 'right' length for such a list is not so much a matter of objective fact, but its convenience to the user. The list we have presented is one which we feel includes the basic factors which need to be considered, without making it so long that it becomes cumbersome. One of the advantages of a checklist as opposed to a complex theory is that it is easy to adapt to suit particular circumstances. Thus, if certain of our factors are of lesser importance in particular jobs they can be omitted without affecting the model as a whole. On the other hand, if other factors not included are important, they can easily be added.

What Can Be Done about It?

Having identified the possible reasons for the performance problem, the checklist next suggests that the manager should review the remedial actions which might be taken to remedy the situation. A number of examples are given in each case.

(i) Goal Clarity

If this is a problem, then some guidance concerning expected standards is called for. According to the situation, this might be a quiet word pointing out that some aspect of performance is important, or a more rigorous goal-setting session with the individual, or some more formal system embracing the whole unit, such as management by objectives.

Research into performance appraisal at the General Electric Co.[7] showed that setting specific performance goals had a greater beneficial effect on subsequent performance than anything else a manager did in performance appraisal interviews. Whilst participation in goal setting had some beneficial effect, a much more powerful influence was whether goals were set at all. Far superior results were observed when *specific* goals were set than when the manager and subordinate merely discussed the needed improvement. Similarly, a number of research studies suggest that individuals who are given, or set themselves, goals which are both hard and specific, achieve higher levels of performance than those who are simply asked to 'do their best'.[8] In a recent survey of the effectiveness of various different methods of performance improvement, Locke and his associates reviewed a total of seventeen studies of goal setting.[9] Performance was improved in all seventeen cases, the increases ranging from 2%–57%, with a median performance improvement of 16%.

(ii) Ability

If the individual's low performance is the result of the lack of some necessary skill or knowledge, and it appears that he or she is capable of acquiring it, then some kind of 'learning experience' is a possible solution to the problem. This might be a formal training course (most often favoured) but other possibilities are transfers or secondments to other departments where the ability can be acquired, time allocated in the present job to practice skills which have gone 'rusty', or personal coaching by the job-holder's own boss. The latter demands the greatest investment of the boss's time and effort, and is probably also the least used.

(iii) Task Difficulty

If the individual appears incapable of acquiring the necessary skills and knowledge for effective task performance, or training would be too expensive or difficult to arrange, then instead of increasing the job-holder's abilities, it may be more appropriate either to replace the job-holder with someone who is more capable of doing the job or to reduce the difficulty of the job to the level where the present job-holder can handle it effectively. The latter might be achieved by simplifying the task, reducing the workload or reducing the time pressure in some way. For example, if a typist is continually unable to produce work in time for deadlines, it might make more sense to reduce time pressure by persuading people to hand work in earlier than to send the typist on a course to increase typing speed. On the other hand, simplifying the task too much can lead to boredom and therefore lower performance. Thus, one may successfully solve an ability problem by task simplification but produce an even worse motivational problem as a result. This leads us to the next item.

(iv) Intrinsic Motivation

Given that people differ widely in the needs which they regard as being important, it follows that to solve a motivational problem the first necessity is to understand the particular needs which are most important to the individual concerned at the time in question. People have such a wide variety of needs that one cannot hope to satisfy them all. In addition, there are many needs which cannot be satisfied easily or practically within the organizational context. Thus what the manager needs to discover is the need which the individual would most like to be fulfilled *next*, and is within the manager's, or the organization's power to fulfil.

If the needs which are most important to the individual are intrinsic to the job, then some form of job redesign is called for. A manager cannot simply give a subordinate such 'rewards' as a sense of achievement, increased self-esteem, or an interest in the job for its own sake. All that can be done is to provide people with the opportunity of experiencing such things by changing the content of the job so that *it* provides more responsibility, more challenge, and intrinsically interesting work.

The evidence from the survey by Locke and his associates suggests that this too can be an effective method of improving work performance.[10] Thirteen studies of job enrichment were reviewed. There was an improvement in performance in twelve cases, the increases ranging from -1% to 63%, with a median performance improvement of 17%.

Nevertheless, there has been an increasing awareness in recent years that job enrichment is not an ideal solution to motivational problems for all employees. Job enrichment often provides a more interesting job at the expense of reduced opportunities for social interaction. The evidence suggests that workers with high social needs may find this 'trade-off' unacceptable.[11] Similarly, the aim of many job enrichment programmes is to give the worker increased responsibility, which is no doubt something which many people value. Others, however, may take the view that unless the increased responsibility is matched by a commensurate increase in pay, management is simply trying to trick them into doing a more difficult job for the same money.

In more recent approaches to job design, therefore, much more attention has been paid to the crucial question of individual differences in motivation. Where jobs are routine and interdependent there is little scope for designing jobs to fit the needs of individual workers. Nevertheless, Hackman and Oldham's Job Diagnostic Survey provides a means of assessing the needs of groups of workers doing the same job, to establish whether there is a general interest in the intrinsic rewards which an enriched job would provide.[12] Research by Hackman, Oldham and others has shown that employees with a high need for intrinsic rewards do in fact respond more positively to complex and stimulating jobs in terms of their satisfaction, motivation and performance.[13] Where jobs are more flexible and independent, there is much that the individual manager can do to allocate responsibilities between subordinates in such a way that they more closely match the subordinate's own particular needs. As noted in Chapter 1, research by Oldham shows that this too is an effective motivational strategy.[14]

(v) Extrinsic Motivation

Where extrinsic rewards are more important to the individual, then we would argue that low motivation is symptomatic of the fact that the individual does not believe that the rewards are commensurate with the effort which is required to achieve them. The problem may be the size of the rewards or the fact that they are not contingent on performance. Many organizational rewards are at most only partially at the disposal of the individual manager, e.g. salary increments, promotion. Nevertheless, we believe that the extrinsic rewards which are available to the individual manager are both under and inappropriately used. Managers often complain that they lack the extrinsic rewards at their disposal to encourage good performance. Yet, if it is suggested to these same managers that most organizations use an inverse reward systems, punishing good performance and rewarding poor, they will agree and quote numerous examples from their own experience. Poor performance on a disliked task is 'rewarded' by being taken off it; good performance is 'punished' by being given more of the same. People who continually cause conflict are treated with deference and rarely asked to do disliked tasks, because of the unpleasantness which will ensue, and are given 'perks' to placate them. People who get on with their work without any fuss are ignored. It sometimes appears that extrinsic reward systems could not more effectively encourage poor performance if they were designed to do so.

We would suggest, therefore, that if managers feel that their staff lack extrinsic motivation, they should examine all the rewards that they have at their disposal—verbal recognition, more interesting work assignments, not being given last minute onerous assignments, time off, visits to conferences, salary and promotion recommendations, and so on—and then ask themselves whether these go to good performers or to poor performers. If the latter, or there is little difference, then it is hardly surprising that their staff lack extrinsic motivation. To help in the analysis we recommend that they fill in a simple diagram (Figure 2). If most of the items are in quadrants 2 and 3, then there is something wrong with the reward system and it should be realigned to give rewards for good performance and negative or at least zero outcomes for poor.

As we noted in Chapter 1, there is research evidence that rewarding good performance by giving recognition and merit increases does lead to good performance. Similarly, Locke and his associates' survey of performance improvement methods examined 15 different studies of the payment by results system and found that performance improved in all 15 cases. The range of improvement was 3% to 75% with a median of 35%.[15]

Performance

	Good	Poor
Positive	1	2
Negative	3	4

FIGURE 2 Extrinsic Rewards and Work Performance

Finally, it is worth noting that although we have dealt with intrinsic and extrinsic motivation separately for reasons of convenience, many people will have important unfulfilled needs in both areas. For these people, rather than looking exclusively at either intrinsic or extrinsic rewards, it will be more appropriate to seek ways of achieving an acceptable balance between the two.[16] One of the most common reasons for the failure of job enrichment programmes, for example, has been the fact that extrinsic rewards have been ignored. Jobs have been enriched by building into them more challenge and responsibility, but pay levels have been left unchanged. As noted earlier, this has led to dissatisfaction on the part of the workers concerned who felt, not surprisingly, that their pay should be increased commensurate with their new responsibilities.[17]

(vi) Feedback

If this is a problem, then the provision of some form of feedback is necessary. Care must be taken in deciding how this is done. The trainer or manager may have little difficulty distinguishing between negative feedback and punishment, but the distinction may not be so apparent to the trainee or subordinate. Nevertheless, handled well, feedback can have a major impact on performance. At Emery Air Freight, for example, customer service employees believed that they were responding to customer enquiries within 90 minutes nine times out of ten. The company instituted a feedback system whereby the employees monitored and logged their own performance. It was found that the 90 minutes response time was actually being met only three times out of ten. Supervisors periodically inspected the records and gave praise when performance improved, but simply ignored the results when there was no improvement. Similar techniques were used in other areas, such as container utilization and delivery driving. The improved performance achieved by this combination of feedback and recognition is estimated to have saved Emery Air Freight two million dollars over a three-year period.[18]

(vii) Resources

If the problem is genuinely one of inadequate resources, then as far as possible the necessary additional staff, equipment or raw materials should be provided. If this is not possible, then the adverse effects on morale may make the effective handling of motivation an even more important priority.

On the other hand, it is as well to check carefully whether inadequate resources do constitute the real problem. It is all too easy for an individual or group of people to focus on salient factors such as pay or equipment as a major cause of their feelings of discontent. The salesman may blame his lack of success on his ageing, unimpressive car or the scientist may blame the cramped, old-fashioned laboratories. Both complaints could be valid. However, it may be that there are other, less obvious sources of discontent behind these complaints, dissatisfaction or frustrations which are not expressed because they are more difficult to crystallize or express. Improving resources can then have the opposite effect to that intended. The salesman has his new car and the scientist a spacious new laboratory and yet they still feel dissatisfied. Furthermore, they have now lost the one thing which gave them hope, the thought that things would be better once they had the new equipment they needed. Paradoxically, therefore, the result of apparently fulfilling their needs could be a sudden and drastic drop in morale rather than an increase. This is, of course, not an excuse for doing nothing about complaints concerning inadequate resources, but is rather a plea for finding out whether inadequate resources are the genuine, or indeed only, source of the dissatisfaction.

(viii) Working Conditions

As with resources, complaints about working conditions may simply represent something to 'gripe' about or may be the symptom of some deeper source of dissatisfaction which is difficult to crystalize or express. Again, therefore, it is a good idea to check whether working conditions are the real or the only source of the problem.

Nevertheless, poor working conditions can genuinely have adverse effects on work performance, health and safety. There are a great many regulations concerning minimum acceptable standards with respect to certain aspects of working conditions, such as illumination, temperature, rest pauses. Nevertheless, there is often much that managers can still do to ensure improved working conditions, once these have been established as a genuine problem. Minimum acceptable standards are rarely optimum requirements, and working conditions are not only important in themselves, but are also indicative of a company's concern towards its employees.

Before leaving the factors influencing work performance, one further point is worth noting. For ease of presentation, it has been assumed that performance problems tend to arise because people lack something, e.g. ability, motivation, resources, and that the solution to the problem consists of finding some way of increasing such variables. However, this may not always be the case. Sometimes, too much of one of these variables may adversely affect performance. If the individual's abilities are too high for the task then he or she may become bored and careless. If motivation is too high it may cause anxiety which will prevent an employee from making the best use of his or her abilities. If resources are too plentiful, a manager may spend valuable time managing resources rather than working towards the achievement of objectives, and so on.

In some cases, such problems will be picked up under other headings in the checklist. For example, 'too much ability' would reveal itself as 'lack of intrinsic motivation' and 'too many resources' as 'task too difficult', and so on. Nevertheless, when using the checklist, it is worth remembering that a performance problem may occasionally arise because there is too much of one of these performance variables rather than too little. Therefore, rather than trying to maximize each variable, one should try to achieve an optimum level, and this will vary from job to job and person to person. For example, high levels of anxiety are less likely to have adverse effects on performance of simple tasks. Similarly, one individual may be able to work well under pressure whilst another may not, or one individual may like tightly defined objectives whilst another feels that this constrains his or her area of discretion. Thus, when attempting to solve performance problems, it should be remembered that we are never dealing with either the characteristics of the job or the characteristics of the job-holder alone, but with the relationship between them.

What More Do I Need to Know?

So far, then, the manager has generated a list of hypotheses regarding *possible* reasons for and solutions to a performance problem. The next stage is to narrow these possible solutions down to an action plan—those relatively small number of steps which are actually going to be taken to solve the problem.

It may be that the manager already has sufficient information at his or her fingertips to select immediately an appropriate solution. Unless the problem is very straightforward, however, the manager is likely to require further information, either to check the validity of his or her hypotheses or to check whether there might not be other plausible hypotheses to be considered. This information might be obtained by, for example, consulting records, observing the individual's work behaviour or, probably most useful of all, talking to the person concerned. In addition, the manager may wish to talk to any other people involved to check out their feelings about the validity, feasibility or acceptability of the solution. In addition to diagnostic skills, these information gathering processes will require observational and interpersonal skills, which we will discuss later.

What is the Best Solution?

Having collected any additional information required, the checklist next suggests that the manager should select the most appropriate solution(s), and if it is worthwhile in cost–benefit terms, then arrange for its/their implementation. It is worth re-examining the value of the solutions achieved at this stage, because there is a danger that the manager may have become so involved in the problem that he or she is determined to implement the 'perfect' solution, even though it may cost more than the problem deserves and perhaps cause problems elsewhere in the system.

If the solution is not worthwhile in cost–benefit terms, then there are a number of options open. One could work through the checklist again looking for a better solution, relocate the individual, reorganize the whole department or organization, or learn to live with the problem. However, we would argue that drastic steps like relocating the individual or reorganizing the unit, should not be done until all possible measures to improve the individual's performance have been taken. Also, the knowledge that one has taken all the measures possible may help one to live with the problem if there is no other alternative.

Do I Deserve a Pat on the Back?

Finally, we suggest that the manager should review his or her own performance in attempting to solve the problem, and ask whether it could have been tackled better. If so, then this is also a performance problem which might benefit from being analyzed in terms of the checklist. Was it unclear objectives, lack of ability or motivation which resulted in an unacceptable level of performance, and, if so, what should be done about it?

The Checklist in Practice

It must be stressed that the aim of the checklist is not to enable managers to come to any final conclusions regarding the solution to a performance problem.

As we have already noted, further information will often be required, which will involve other skills in addition to diagnostic ones. The aim instead is to provide a means of thinking a problem over before collecting any further information, in order to clarify one's thoughts, decide precisely what information is required, and perhaps also to provide guidelines for a discussion with the person concerned. Rather than single solutions which can be implemented without further consideration, the objective is to help managers to generate a *wider* range of hypotheses concerning the possible reasons for and solutions to performance problems than they otherwise would. Unless a wide variety of possible causes and solutions are considered, there is always a danger that a key factor in the situation may be overlooked and as a result the manager will too quickly accept an 'obvious' but invalid explanation and impose an inadequate solution.

The checklist does appear to fulfil this function. We have used it with managers and management students who have analyzed either vignettes developed by the authors[19] or 'real life' problems from their own experience. What typically happens is that, starting from a small number of symptoms, participants generate a wider variety of possible reasons and an even wider variety of possible solutions. This was confirmed in a study which we carried out with 42 second year undergraduate Business Studies students. The control group was simply given a vignette of the type presented at the beginning of this chapter and asked to list possible reasons for and possible solutions to the performance problem. The experimental group were first given the checklist and a short talk explaining its rationale, before analyzing the problem. In both groups, subjects analyzed the problem individually, and were given 40 minutes to produce their answers. The experimental group produced significantly more possible reasons and solutions than the control group.[20]

CONCLUSIONS

At the beginning of this chapter, we asked you to suggest possible reasons for Geoff's inadequate performance and actions which could be taken to improve the situation. In Figure 3, we show some of the reasons and solutions which might be generated using the checklist. These are, of course, not the only possible answers, nor are they necessarily 'better' than any other list which might be developed. However, it does show the wide variety of ideas which can be generated starting from a very small number of symptoms.

To managers who pride themselves upon being hard-headed realists, distrustful of the 'humanitarian' approaches of behavioural scientists, this may seem a great deal of trouble to take over a 20 year old draughtsman. Would it not be much simpler and less time-consuming merely to call him in, tell him he has to mend his ways and sack him if his performance does not improve? In the end it may, in effect, come to this, but then Geoff will have to be replaced, the post advertised, applicants interviewed, the new draughtsman selected and put

Possible Reasons For Performance Problem	Possible Solutions
Goal clarity Geoff does not realize how important it is that drawings are completed on time	Let Geoff know that completing drawings on time is essential. Set targets, e.g. not less than 9 out of 10 drawings shall be completed within the specified time
Ability Geoff lacks the drawing skills to produce adequate plans both quickly and accurately	Give him advice on drawing techniques (e.g. short-cuts which will enable him to work more quickly) Find out whether there is a suitable training course
Task difficulty The architects are not giving Geoff long enough deadlines. All four of them give their own work top priority. Geoff has given up trying to achieve these deadlines because he knows they are impossible	Get the architects to schedule their work better so that Geoff is either given longer deadlines or work which is more evenly spread.
Intrinsic motivation Geoff finds simply producing fair copies of other peoples' rough sketches boring. He doesn't even know what the plans are **for** in most cases	Enrich Geoff's job in some way, e.g. allow him to attend meetings or discussions at an earlier stage in the planning and design process so that he feels more involved in the work
Extrinsic motivation Geoff never receives any recognition when his drawings **are** on time. When they are late people grumble, but nothing else seems to happen	Train the architects to praise Geoff when drawings are on time. If there are any specific positive or negative outcomes which can result from good or bad performance point these out to Geoff, then make sure they occur or lose credibility
Feedback Geoff knows he is late occasionally but does not realize how often or the disruptive effect this has	Institute a feedback system showing how many plans are on time and how many are late and by how much
Resources Geoff's equipment is old fashioned and cumbersome, unsuitable for fast, accurate work	Provide better equipment
Working conditions Geoff's working environment is both hot and noisy, the main noise coming from the typing pool next door, which he finds very distracting. He is also the only person in his badly ventilated room and feels very isolated	Improve ventilation and sound proofing, involve him more in the work of the architects

FIGURE 3 Improving Geoff's Performance: Some Hypotheses Concerning the Reasons for Inadequate Performance and Possible Solutions

through the induction process. Going through the checklist concerning Geoff's performance and interviewing him about it is likely to take little more time than preparing for and carrying out a *single* selection interview. At least, this will be true if the selection interviews are carried out thoroughly, and there is little point in sacking Geoff unless one makes a better job of selection next time. Thus sacking Geoff and replacing him could be much more time-consuming than improving his performance, with no guarantee that it will solve the problem.

Similarly it could be argued that the performance of a 20 year old draughtsman is a rather trivial problem, hardly worth dignifying with such a term as leadership. However, marginally substandard performers like Geoff are very common in organizations, *at all levels*, and dealing with their problems and improving their performance *is* efficient and economic management of people, and that is what leadership is really about.

In this chapter, we have discussed the development of hypotheses concerned with improving performance at work. In the following chapters we shall look at techniques for narrowing these hypotheses down to an action plan.

EXERCISE 1

Read the following case, and using the checklist described in this chapter, list what you think might be the reasons for the performance problem(s) and the actions which might be taken to improve the situation.

Michael's Prospects

Michael Jones is a research scientist in the synthetic goods division of Allibar Ltd. He joined them four years ago after obtaining his PhD. Allibar counted themselves very lucky to be able to recruit him. He has a first class honours degree, his PhD research was in an area very relevant to Allibar's interests and his university referees predicted that he could have had a brilliant academic future had he not chosen to go into industry. Since joining Allibar he has gained the reputation of being one of their most creative research scientists. Not only has he made a number of important breakthrough's in his own research area, but he also seems to have the happy knack of being able to come up with creative suggestions which help colleagues to get round bottlenecks in their own projects.

Michael has heard that a section managership is likely to become vacant through internal transfer. He therefore asks his own section manager whether she thinks he will get the job. He suggests that his record with the company should make him front runner for the post. Sheila agrees with him that his scientific reputation in the company is second to none for someone of his age and experience, and he could certainly expect to be promoted to senior research scientist in the not too distant future. However, she adds that there is more to research administration than being a brilliant scientist, and the one thing which could hold him back from becoming a section manager and progressing further in research management was his lack of foresight. "Let me give you an example", she says. "Thanks to your scientific breakthrough we can now produce synthetic beefsteak which is virtually indistinguishable in texture from the real thing, but there was a delay of two months during the project whilst we were waiting for essential new materials to arrive and a delay of another month at the end whilst we were waiting for the consumer tests to be arranged. Both these things cost the company money, Mike, and they could have been foreseen. They might even have let a competitor get on the market ahead of us in some cases.'' ''That's not fair,'' said Mike ''I was concentrating on the scientific side. I leave that kind of thing to my Research Assistant. I thought he'd arranged things.'' ''But it is a section manager's responsibility to ensure that delays like these don't happen, and if you are going to progress as a research manager you will have to demonstrate an improvement in this area. What we need to do is to work out why it was that your advance planning wasn't adequate and what we can do about it. Then perhaps I might feel happier recommending you for a section managers job.''

A 'model' answer to this exercise is given in Appendix I.

NOTES AND REFERENCES

1 EH Schein (1965), *Organizational Psychology*, Prentice-Hall.

2 NRF Maier (1955), *Psychology in Industry*, Harrap.

3 JP Campbell and RD Pritchard (1976), 'Motivation Theory in Industrial and Organizational Psychology', in Dunnette, MD, *Handbook of Industrial and Organizational Psychology*, Rand McNally.

4 RF Mager and P Pipe (1970), *Analysing Performance Problems*, Fearon Publishers.

5 For more detailed information on working conditions see, for example, EJ McCormick and D Ilgen (1980), *Industrial Psychology*, 7th edn., Prentice-Hall.

6 Campbell and Pritchard (1976), *op. cit.*

7 HH Meyer, E Kay and JR French (1965), 'Split Roles in Performance Appraisal', *Harvard Business Review*, Vol. 43, pp. 123–129.

8 EA Locke (1968), 'Toward a Theory of Task Motivation and Incentives', *Organizational Behaviour and Human Performance*, Vol. 3, pp. 157–189.
   EA Locke, KN Shaw, LM Saari and GP Latham (1981), 'Goal Setting and Task Performance: *1969–1980*', *Psychological Bulletin*, Vol. 90, pp. 125–152.

9 EA Locke, DB Feren, VM McCaleb, KN Shaw and AT Denny (1980), 'The Relative Effectiveness of Four Methods of Motivating Employee Performance', in K Duncan, M Gruneberg and D Wallis, (eds), *Changes in Working Life*, John Wiley.

10 Locke, *et al.* (1980), *op. cit.*

11 WE Reif and F Luthans (1972), 'Does Job Enrichment Really Pay Off?', *California Management Review*, Vol. 15, pp. 30–37.

12 JR Hackman and GR Oldham (1975), 'Development of the Job Diagnostic Survey,' *Journal of Applied Psychology*, Vol. 60, pp. 159–170.

13 JR Hackman and GR Oldham (1976), 'Motivation through Design of Work: Test of a Theory', *Organizational Behaviour and Human Performance*, Vol. 16, pp. 250–279.
   JR Hackman, JL Pierce and JC Wolfe (1978), 'Effects of Changes in Job Characteristics on Work Attitudes and Behaviours: A Naturally Occurring Quasi-experiment', *Organizational Behaviour and Human Performance*, Vol. 21, pp. 289–304.

14 GR Oldham (1976), 'The Motivational Strategies Used by Supervisors: Relationships to Effectiveness Indicators', *Organizational Behaviour and Human Performance*, Vol. 15, pp. 66–86.

15 Locke, *et al.* (1980), *op. cit.*

16 It has been suggested, principally by Deci, that intrinsic and extrinsic rewards conflict with each other, and thus the introduction of contingent extrinsic rewards would reduce the individual's level of intrinsic motivation. However, later reviews of the research literature, for example by Scott and Greaves, indicate that this is an oversimplification, particularly in the working environment. Thus there appears to be no reason why steps should not be taken to increase levels of intrinsic and extrinsic motivation at the same time. See EL Deci (1971), 'Effects of Externally Mediated Rewards on Intrinsic Motivation', *Journal of Personality and Social Psychology*, Vol. 18, pp. 105–115; WE Scott (1975), 'The Effects of Extrinsic Rewards on "Intrinsic Motivation": A Critique', *Organizational Behaviour and Human Performance*, Vol. 15, pp. 117–129; R Greaves (1978), 'Intrinsic and Extrinsic Motivation—Cooperation or Conflict: A Critical Review', unpublished MBA dissertation, University of Bradford Management Centre.

17 See EE Lawler (1977), 'Reward Systems', in JR Hackman and JL Suttle, (eds), *Improving Life at Work*, Goodyear, pp. 222–223.

18 EJ Feeney (1972), 'Performance Audit, Feedback and Positive Reinforcement', *Training and Development Journal*, Vol. 26, pp. 8–13.

19 PL Wright and DS Taylor (1981), 'Vignette Analysis as an Aid to Psychology Teaching', *Bulletin of the British Psychological Society*, Vol. 34, pp. 57–60.

20 DS Taylor and PL Wright (1982), 'Influencing Work Performance: The Development of Diagnostic Skills', *Journal of Management Development*, Vol. 1, pp. 44–50.

Chapter 3

Perception and Judgement

Peter Broadbent is *inspecting* the current sales figures. He is gratified to *see* that overall sales have increased. On *checking* further, however, he *notices* that the increase is made up entirely of new sales and that repeat orders have in fact declined slightly. He *decides* to *check* further, and *discovers* that one member of the sales staff in particular, Mary Burton, has brought in a great deal of new business, but not maintained sales with existing customers. He *decides* to talk to her about it and arranges a meeting. During the meeting, he *notices* that Mary seems ill at ease when discussing repeat sales, and asks her whether she has any particular problems in this area. She replies that she probably has not given them as much attention as she should—they are a lot less exciting to her than going out and getting new business—but she had been surprised and concerned at the large drop in repeat sales in the last set of figures and had resolved to give them more attention in future. Peter and Mary then agree objectives for the next sales period, both in terms of time to be spent on repeat sales and new business, and expected sales in these areas, and Peter says he will be *keeping an eye* on her performance in these areas during this period and will discuss the matter further with her when the next sales figures are available.

INTRODUCTION

The ability to make accurate inferences concerning the factors which determine peoples' behaviour and events is one of the key skills of management. In the previous chapter, we outlined some of the main factors which influence work performance. However, a mere knowledge of these factors is not sufficient in itself to identify the specific causes of someone's behaviour in a particular instance, or to decide what should be done to change his or her future behaviour in a desired direction. Accurate perception and judgement are also required. They play a vital role, not only in the initial analysis of a performance problem, but also at several other stages during an attempt to influence behaviour at work.

This is illustrated in the case at the beginning of this chapter. Peter Broadbent notices a discrepancy in the sales figures. From this he infers that there may be a performance problem. He gathers further information which pinpoints a possible source of the problem. He talks to the person concerned and gathers more information both from what she says and from her nonverbal behaviour. Steps are agreed which are intended to remedy the situation, and the manager resolves to observe the subordinate's performance more carefully in future. Various skills are required at different stages during this process, such as the ability to analyze performance problems and to gather information and arrive at decisions with subordinates. Throughout the event as a whole, however, the manager is using and relying on his ability to perceive and interpret situations accurately in order to provide the basis for a series of decisions. This process is illustrated in Figure 4.

At any particular time, a wide variety of information is available to the manager within his or her working environment. Certain pieces of information may be noticed or sought out by the manager, often those which experience indicates are important in his or her job. Simply perceiving what has happened does not, however, provide an adequate basis for action. The same events could have entirely different implications depending on the circumstances. The information must be evaluated, consciously or unconsciously to establish its meaning as clearly as the available data permits.[1] A decision is then made, either deliberately or by default, to clarify the situation by gathering further information, or to take action on the basis of existing data, or to do nothing. Whichever action the manager takes will have consequences to be perceived, interpreted, and form the basis of future decisions. Thus we are concerned with a continual perception–judgement–decision-making cycle.

Judgement and decision-making are pervasive and continuous activities. For the most part, people are successful in dealing with a wide range of problems. However, failures in the perception and interpretation of information do occur, which can have adverse effects on decision-making, particularly where there is also a failure to check the immediate consequences of the decisions. Such failures can occur for a number of reasons:

Selective perception—a person may fail to perceive some or all of the required information.

Distortions of perception—a person may perceive the information but because of the situation or context in which it is presented, perceive it incorrectly.

Incorrect Interpretation—a person may perceive the information correctly but misinterpret its meaning or significance.

These sources of error will now be looked at in more detail.

SELECTIVE PERCEPTION

In our everyday environment there are thousands of sources of information. Purposeful behaviour is impossible unless we select from all these information sources, or stimuli, those that have relevance for our interests, needs and intentions, shutting ourselves off from those that are irrelevant. We are limited in how much we can attend to, so selectivity is essential.

We do not respond at random to objects or events in our environment,

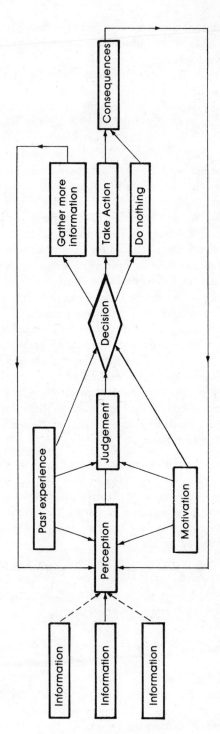

FIGURE 4 Perception and Judgement at Work

several factors can affect our selection. These can be included under three broad headings: the nature of the object or event, our past experience and our intentions or motives.

The Nature of the Object or Event

In our everyday living, some objects and events attract our attention, that is, they select themselves. These include objects and events associated with loud noises, bright lights, strong smells, sudden or rapid movement—they contrast strongly with other stimuli in the environment. That such stimuli can demand attention has significant survival value because they often signal important events, and as such they are often used purposely in our society. For example, sirens and flashing lights announce emergency vehicles. Bright or decorative clothing is often worn to attract members of the opposite sex. Advertisers use flashing lights and huge displays etc. to catch our attention. Similar attention-demanding stimuli are also used in the organizational environment. Loud noises and bright or flashing lights signal danger, emergency, or breakdown of equipment. More subtly, but no less effectively, contrasting dress is used to announce status. Our attention is immediately drawn to the smartly suited boss among his overalled employees or the overalled supervisor among blue boiler suited operators.

The same contrasting effects are often used purposely by people to attract attention to themselves. Someone who is brightly dressed, uses flamboyant gestures, talks loudly or 'darts' quickly about is much more likely to be noticed than someone who dresses drably or behaves in a restrained or quiet manner. These characteristics, however, are not necessarily correlated with work performance. The person who talks loudly about his or her achievements may well contribute much less to the organization's performance than the nondescript, retiring person who quietly gets on with essential work. However, evidence[2] indicates that when organizational rewards are being considered, the former is much more likely to be remembered and rewarded than the latter, strongly indicating that the more conspicuous is a potential contributor, then the greater the causal role that will be assigned to that person for particular results or events.

In general, the more striking or vivid information is, the more likely it is to be attended to, and as a result remembered. Information that is easily remembered is then more likely to be recalled at some later relevant time and influence interpretation, evaluation and judgement.

Past Experience

It follows from the previous section that, other things being equal, stimuli which are *less* intense, smaller, contrast little with what has gone before, and move slowly or not at all, are *less* likely to be noticed. Nevertheless, such stimuli can be extremely important, and we do often pay attention to them. A slight deflection of the needle on a dial may indicate that a complex piece of equipment is malfunctioning, or a slight frown may indicate, if we are sufficiently observant, that our attempt at persuasive communication is failing. What is it then that determines which of these low level stimuli is attended to and which is ignored?

One factor is past experience. In general, we perceive things we are used to seeing more readily than those we are not. Someone seeing the well known illustration below for the first time would very likely see "Paris in the spring", because that is the type of construction they are used to seeing.

Similar effects can occur in the perception of people's behaviour at work. It may take us longer to notice behaviour which is 'out of character'. For example, signs of stubbornness and rejection on the part of a usually compliant subordinate may be ignored at first, leading us to persist with an inappropriate method of handling the situation. On the other hand, with a normally 'difficult' subordinate, the first indication of lack of acceptance is likely to be registered immediately. In this case, it is signs of compliance which may not register immediately, leading the manager to continue pushing his or her views long after the message has been accepted.

The same considerations apply in interpersonal interactions, with respect to the expression of needs. Usually, although not always, all of us can recognize needs which are shouted at us in a simple form (e.g. *"If I don't get a rise I shall hand in my notice"* or *"How can you expect me to achieve the set quotas with old machinery that frequently breaks down?"*). However, needs which are expressed obliquely, briefly or quietly whilst discussing other things are all too easy to miss. Again, this is particularly so when they are unexpected, as for example when a highly competent worker expresses doubts about his or her abilities. The strength with which such needs are expressed may bear little relationship to their importance to the individual expressing them. Once the apparently satisfied worker has suffered a breakdown, the warning signs may be quite clear in retrospect, but by then of course it is too late. Hindsight is an exact science, but it is foresight that is essential for effective management. To be more effective in this area, probably the first point to recognize is that people tend to be overconfident in their judgements and are more certain in their beliefs, evaluations and theories than close analysis would probably justify. Further, this is more likely to occur when making judgements, expressing beliefs, or evaluating people rather than physical things. If this is recognized, and one can also recognize that the same events, behaviour or data might easily be interpreted from the basis of different beliefs or theories, then a less determined stance might be taken, and one in which further information will be gathered to check on one's inference, interpretation or evaluation.

Motivation

The third factor which may determine which stimuli are perceived or ignored is self interest. Again, this is well known to advertisers who attempt to attract our attention by including in their adverts things which are likely to interest us, whether they are directly related to their product or not.

Within the organizational context too, our personal pattern of needs, interests, beliefs and attitudes will affect our selection and interpretation of information. An engineer and a personnel manager being shown around a factory are likely to attend to, and seek out, information about different aspects of the operator–machine production system, relating to their interests and expertise. Furthermore, each one in his or her own area of expertise is likely to see more than the other. So for example, the personnel manager may detect hostility between two operators by their body orientations and mannerisms, points which even if brought to the attention of the engineer may be difficult to perceive. Similarly the engineer can point out machine operations to the non-engineer, which may be difficult to discriminate or understand. That is, people uneducated or without experience in areas of specialization may be unable to perceive particular aspects of the situation even when their attention is drawn to them.

Our beliefs and attitudes will also influence to what we attend and therefore 'register' and remember. Differences in beliefs and attitudes between union officers and management or subordinates and managers have implications for organizational behaviour. The manager probably ignores instances in which a subordinate is effectively working without supervision but quickly notices a subordinate 'hanging about' smoking. His or her belief that workers are lazy and therefore need constant supervision causes the selection of those instances which reinforce his or her views and non-selection of disconfirming instances.

PERCEPTUAL DISTORTION

So far we have been discussing factors which determine whether people, objects or events are perceived or not. Sometimes however, we perceive things but perceive them inaccurately. There are many instances in which those factors which relate to selective perception can also 'distort' perception, or arrange it so that we 'see' what we are used to seeing or expect to see. In a way, each of us reconstructs or distorts the world to our own liking based on needs, beliefs, expectations and so on, even though we are in intimate interaction with our immediate environment.

The Nature of the Object or Event

As might be expected, objects or events which are most likely to be misinterpreted are those which are ambiguous or cannot be clearly perceived because they are faint, distant, experienced in adverse conditions, occur very briefly or unexpectedly, and so on. As we shall see, however, this does not prevent people from forming clear and unambiguous impressions of such objects and events, sometimes leading to false conclusions or conflict with other people whose impressions are quite different, but equally clear and unambiguous. Eyewitness testimony provides many examples of this process. For example, practically every car accident results in wide variations between witnesses regarding how fast the cars were travelling and the sequence of events leading up to the accident. There are also cases in which witnesses are willing to testify that they saw something which has subsequently been shown to be impossible. In one case, a police officer testified that he saw a defendant shoot a victim as both stood in a doorway 120 feet away. Members of the jury on going to the scene of the crime found it impossible to identify the features of a person standing in the doorway from that distance and acquitted the defendant.[3]

Past Experience

Knowledge from past experience is essential for perception to occur. It enables us to recognize and categorize information much more rapidly, and thus react much more quickly to what we perceive. Therein, however, lies a danger. If the knowledge is incorrect or the past experience misleading, we may misinterpret the stimulus and react on the basis of incorrect information. Once such a premature categorization has been made, it is often very resistant to change, as any new information which could provide contradictory evidence is often distorted to fit existing beliefs.

A classic example is the case of eight researchers who voluntarily admitted themselves to American mental hospitals complaining of voices which said "empty", "hollow" and "thud". Immediately after admission to the psychiatric ward, these pseudopatients ceased simulating any symptoms of abnormality. They behaved normally and when asked by staff how they were feeling, they replied that they were fine and no longer experienced any symptoms. Nevertheless, none of them were detected, and they were discharged from the hospitals with a diagnosis of schizophrenia "in remission", i.e. in the hospital's view, the patient still had schizophrenia but was not showing signs of it at the moment. Oddly enough, the people who did notice the deception were other patients, who would say things like "You're not crazy. You're a journalist or a professor. You're checking up on the hospital". At first, the researchers took notes secretly, but they soon found that this was unnecessary. Even their note taking was seen as pathological behaviour, such as compulsive writing. As far as the doctors were concerned, once a diagnosis of schizophrenia had been made, everything they subsequently learned about the patient, no matter how innocuous, was interpreted as supporting the original diagnosis.[4]

The above case involves the formal categorizing of people in terms of medical diagnosis. Nevertheless, the more subtle, informal and sometimes unconscious categorizing of people which occurs in everyday life can still have profound effects on the judgements we make about people. As Anastasi[5] points out, some hunches we have about people may result from a chance resemblance to a former acquaintance. If a previous employee who embezzled funds also happened to have widely spaced eyes then a manager might experience vague feelings of distrust whenever encountering someone with widely spaced eyes, without even realizing the basis of these feelings. Some common sources of distortion in assessing people are as follows.

1. First Impressions

We often form lasting impressions of people on the basis of limited information gained during a very brief period after we have first encountered them. In selection interviews, for example, impressions of the candidate are commonly crystallized by the end of the first four minutes.[6] Once formed, our first impressions are maintained by interpreting all subsequent information in terms of our initial conclusions. Thus we can never be wrong, at least in our own eyes. 'Blowing the whistle' on a colleague who is behaving unethically can be seen as a sign of integrity or disloyalty, depending upon whether one originally categorized the person concerned as honest or shifty. Similarly, the rapid progress made by recruits identified as 'high flyers' is sometimes quoted as evidence for an organization's ability to identify management potential at an early stage. However, once someone has been identified as a high flyer, it is likely that their subsequent behaviour, unless grossly incompetent, will be interpreted as confirming this initial assessment.

2. The Halo Effect

If a person makes a favourable or unfavourable impression in one area, then this can also affect our impressions of other aspects of the person's personality and behaviour. Thus a person who is seen as friendly, may also be regarded as loyal, trustworthy and intelligent, even though independent evidence concerning these traits is lacking. Similarly, someone who performs well or badly on one particular task may be assumed to be a generally good or poor performer, irrespective of his or her actual performance in other areas. This effect is probably the most pervasive source of error in performance appraisal, where the manager's perception of one or two attributes or events can colour his or her assessment of the subordinate's whole performance. Furthermore, it is highly resistant to elimination. Even the knowledge that one is susceptible to this sort of error may not be sufficient to prevent it. The evidence indicates that only the application of relatively sophisticated statistical control techniques is effective in reducing it.[7]

3. Stereotyping

Stereotypes are beliefs that all members of a particular group possess certain common characteristics or ways of behaving. Racial stereotyping is probably the best known and most pernicious form. Nevertheless, there are stereotypes for almost every class of people—librarians, nurses, managers, shop stewards, professors, people who wear glasses, pin-striped suits, or have beards, people who are thin, fat, old, young, male, female and so on. Many of these stereotypes will influence how we see other people in organizations and perhaps through this influence how we interact with them. Therein lies the danger.

If we have no knowledge of a person whom we are about to meet, information about who that person mixes with and the groups he or she belongs to may help to reduce uncertainty and increase our chances of successfully interacting with that person. However, the critical factor is the assumption that because that person belongs to a particular group he or she will behave according to our stereotype of that group. It could be that the stereotype is in general wrong, being based on false assumptions, or that the individual with whom we are concerned is atypical.

There are many examples of research which indicate that stereotypes affect the perceptual/judgemental process. For example, the more facial scars a person has, the more dishonest that person is judged to be. Physically attractive individuals of both sexes are rated as more warm, responsive, interesting, sociable, kind and poised than less attractive individuals and more likely to attain high occupational status.[8] Where males and females are candidates for jobs, even where both are equally qualified, males are given higher evaluations in general than are females;[9] this effect is greater when the interviewer is highly authoritarian.[10] Even where women were recommended for hiring as frequently as identically qualified men, they were offered significantly lower starting salaries and subsequent pay rises tended to increase the initial salary discrepancy.[11] Sex-role stereotyping seems to influence all facets of occupational life, usually to the disadvantage of women.

Stereotypes are learned from experience. We may encounter a few members of a group who possess some common characteristic and assume, perhaps mistakenly, that all other members of the group share the same characteristic. Alternatively, stereotypes may be acquired by accepting the views of other people without actually encountering any members of the group in question. The stereotype of the absent-minded professor, for example, probably exists amongst many people who have never even met a professor, let alone an absent-minded one.

Once formed, stereotypes can persist for a number of reasons. We may never come across a member of the group in question, or in some cases may not realize that we have done so. Thus we may never encounter any evidence to refute our stereotype. Alternatively, we may give undue weight to cases which do appear to confirm the stereotype, ignoring contradicting evidence or regarding it as "the exception which proves the rule".

The dangers of stereotyping are all too evident. We are not treating people as individuals and consequently our decisions about them may be biassed or wrong. The results of this can include inefficient selection of personnel, poor development of personnel, inadequate problem solving and ineffective interpersonal interactions.

Motivation

Motivation can not only influence whether we perceive something, but also distort our perceptions of those things we do perceive. It is well known in organizations that superiors and subordinates do not always see things in the same way. Research data quoted by Likert[12] showed just how large these differences can be. Figure 5 shows supervisors' and subordinates' perceptions of how much recognition for good work the supervisors give. Such differences could have far reaching effects on the relations between the two groups. If recognition is important to the subordinates then they are likely to feel resentful that their good work goes unnoticed. Conversely, the supervisors are likely to feel that their level of recognition for good work is perfectly adequate, and perhaps resent the subordinate's lack of response to the recognition they receive. Of course, other differences in perception may exist. Superiors and

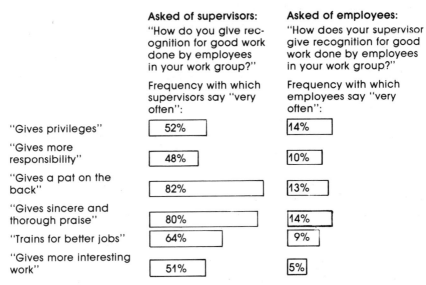

Source: R Likert, **New Patterns of Management**, McGraw-Hill, 1961, p.91

FIGURE 5 Comparison of Supervisors' Description of their Behaviour with Employees' Description of their Experience

subordinates may differ in what they perceive as work good enough to receive recognition, which might account for some of the differences found. Nevertheless, without effective communication between the members of the groups concerned to thrash out what perceptual differences exist and why they occur, they could be a continuing source of frustration and resentment for both parties.

Another study[13] examined how becoming a foreman or union steward affected workers' perceptions of and attitudes towards the company management and the union. Virtually all the 2354 workers of a home appliance company filled in questionnaires concerned with their view of the company, the union and various aspects of the job. Over the next year and a half, 23 workers were made foremen and 35 were elected stewards. Those who became foremen came to see the company as a better place to work compared with other companies, developed more positive perceptions of top management, were more critical of the union, and became more favourably disposed towards the company's incentive scheme. Those who became stewards came to look upon labour unions in general in a more favourable light, developed more positive perceptions of the top union officers at the company, and came to prefer seniority to ability as a criterion for moving workers to better jobs. Furthermore, when 8 of the workers who had been promoted to foremen later reverted back to the shop floor because of an economic recession, their perceptions and attitudes also reverted to those they had held before promotion.

Other research[14] has shown that an individual's role, apart from his or her position in the hierarchy, can influence the way a situation is perceived. A group of 23 executives, all from the same company, were presented with a description of an organization and its activities, and asked to identify the most important problem which it faced. Six of the executives came from Sales, five from Production, and twelve from other departments. The responses of the sales and production executives clearly revealed the influence of the department they worked in. Five of the six sales executives identified sales, marketing or distribution as the main problem, but only one of the five production executives did so. Conversely, four of the five production executives mentioned organizational problems (other than within marketing) as the main problem, whilst only one of the sales executives did so. Only three executives in the group mentioned human relations, employee relations or teamwork as the main problem. Of these, one came from public relations, one from industrial relations and the third from the medical department.

DISTORTION OF JUDGEMENT

It can be very frustrating when we perceive that the path leading to the fulfilment of important needs is blocked, especially if this blockage is also unexpected.[15] Examples might include the discovery of serious errors in a recently typed report just before the deadline for its distribution, a sudden cancellation of an important order by an apparently satisfied customer, the harvest which is ruined by a freak thunderstorm, and so on. As Sanford[16] pointed out, when many millions of people, each seeking satisfaction of his or her own pattern of needs, live in a world which does not bend itself to human desire, then frustration is inevitably a frequent occurrence.

A common initial reaction to such events is shocked disbelief, a denial that the frustrating event has occurred. For example, we may have to read the offending report several times to convince ourselves that the errors are really there! This denial usually fades to be replaced by one or more other reactions to the frustrating situation. Perhaps the most common one, at least in Western cultures, is anger. This may be expressed directly against the frustrating object or person—we may fling the report across the room, abuse the customer for letting us down. Often, however, direct aggression may be inappropriate or inadvisable. It is difficult to attack a thunderstorm, for example, and unwise to attack the customer. Worse still, the source of the frustration may be ourselves, e.g. we may be the person who introduced the serious errors into the report in the first place! Thus, an alternative response, after the initial emotional reaction, is to turn one's energy towards finding a rational solution to the frustrating situation which will alleviate it, or at least make it less likely to recur. If this cannot be done, then we may still be able to accept the situation philosophically, recognizing that disappointments are an inevitable consequence of living in an imperfect world.

Nevertheless, there are times when we find such rational reactions to frustration impossible. Perhaps we are unable to control the anger which has been aroused, or feel extremely anxious about possible future repercussions, or cannot cope with the threat to our self esteem which would result from recognition of our own failings. We may then reduce the sense of frustration and the unpleasant emotions it causes, not by solving the real problem or accepting it philosophically, but by distorting our perception of reality. For example, we may *repress* the memory of the painful event. In time we may conveniently forget that we made a silly mistake which had serious repercussions, and thus retain our self image of alertness and efficiency. We may *displace* our anger on some convenient scapegoat, and 'bawl out' a surprised subordinate for some trivial misdemeanour which would normally have gone unnoticed. We may *project* our unwanted feelings on to other people, saying that it is they, not us, who are aggressive, anxious, ambitious or jealous. Such irrational reactions are called *defence mechanisms* because they serve to protect the individual from the painful emotions which frustration, conflict and anxiety can arouse. A great many others have been identified over the years. A detailed list, together with illustrations from the work environment, was drawn up by Costello and Zalkind[17] and is shown in Table 1.

It should be noted that such defence mechanisms are not invariably maladaptive. If we have to face up to the threatening and distressing events of life immediately and without protection, they could very well overwhelm us. If used on a temporary basis, therefore, defence mechanisms can provide a valuable breathing space during which the apparent severity of the problem is artificially reduced. Then, after the initial emotional impact has faded, we may be able to tackle the problem rationally. On the other hand, defence mechanisms *are* maladaptive when they persist or are over-used. The real problem is often still there, however much one may wish to deny it, and continued use of a defence mechanism may prevent us from finding a permanent, real solution to it. Furthermore, whilst we may manage to fool ourselves by means of defence mechanisms, they often do not fool other people. Thus, in addition to our original problem which remains unsolved, we may also generate a whole new

TABLE 1 Adjustive Reactions to Frustration, Conflict and Anxiety

Adjustive Reactions	Psychological Process	Illustration
Compensation	Individual devotes himself to a pursuit with increased vigour to make up for some feeling of real or imagined inadequacy	Zealous, hard-working president of the Twenty-five Year Club who has never advanced very far in the company hierarchy
Conversion	Emotional conflicts are expressed in muscular, sensory, or bodily symptoms of disability, malfunctioning, or pain	A disabling headache keeping a staff member off the job, the day after a cherished project has been rejected
Displacement	Redirecting pent-up emotions toward persons, ideas, or objects other than the primary source of the emotion	Roughly rejecting a simple request from a subordinate after receiving a rebuff from the boss
Fantasy	Daydreaming or other forms of imaginative activity provides an escape from reality and gives imagined satisfactions	An employee's daydream of the day in the staff meeting when he corrects the boss's mistakes and is publicly acknowledged as the real leader of the industry
Identification	Individual enhances his self esteem by patterning his own behaviour after another's, frequently also internalizing the values and beliefs of the other; also vicariously sharing the glories or suffering in the reversals of other individuals or groups	The 'assistant-to' who takes on the vocabulary, manner-isms, or even pomposity of of his vice-presidential boss
Negativism	Active or passive resistance, operating unconsciously	The manager who, having been unsuccessful in getting out of a committee assignment, picks apart every suggestion that anyone makes in the meetings
Projection	Individual protects himself from awareness of his own undesirable traits or unacceptable feelings by attributing them to others	Unsuccessful person who, deep down, would like to block the rise of others in the organization and who continually feels that others are out to 'get him'
Rationalization	Justifying inconsistent or undesirable behaviour, beliefs, statements and motivations by providing acceptable explanations for them	Padding the expense account because 'everybody does it'

Adjustive Reactions	Psychological Process	Illustration
Reaction-formation	Urges not acceptable to consciousness are re-pressed and in their stead opposite attitudes or modes of behaviour are expressed with considerable force	Employee who has not been promoted who over-does the defence of his boss, vigorously upholding the company's policies
Regression	Individual returns to an earlier and less mature level of adjustment in the face of frustration	A manager having been blocked in some adminis-trative pursuit busies him-self with clerical duties or technical details, more appropriate for his sub-ordinates
Repression	Completely excluding from consciousness impulses, experiences, and feelings which are psychologically disturbing because they arouse a sense of guilt or anxiety	A subordinate 'forgetting' to tell his boss the circum-stances of an embarrassing situation
Fixation	Maintaining a persistent non-adjustive reaction even though all the cues indicate the behaviour will not cope with the problems	Persisting in carrying out an operational procedure long since declared by manage-ment to be uneconomical as a protest because the employee's opinion wasn't asked
Resignation, apathy and boredom	Breaking psychological contact with the environ-ment, withholding any sense of emotional or per-sonal involvement	Employee, who, receiving no reward, praise, or en-couragement, no longer cares whether or not he does a good job
Flight or withdrawal	Leaving the field in which frustration, anxiety or con-flict is experienced, either physically or psycho-logically	The salesman's big order falls through and he takes the rest of the day off; con-stant rebuff or rejection by superiors and colleagues, pushes an older worker toward being a loner and ignoring what friendly gestures are made

Source: TW Costello and SS Zalkind (1963), **Psychology in Administration: A Research Orientation**, Prentice-Hall, pp. 148–149.

set of problems in our relations with people who resent our displaced aggression, inadequate excuses, refusal to 'face the facts', and so on.

However, not all distortion of judgement occurs as a result of frustration. There are many situations in which we have to make predictions and evaluations for reasons other than in reaction to frustration. In these situations where hard information is not available people generally base their evaluations and predictions on the ease with which similar occurrences or examples can be brought to mind. Thus the source of the information for making such judgements is our own memory. The accuracy of the judgements in these cases will be affected by how representative of reality our memories are. This chapter has highlighted many factors which can bias attention and perception and, as a result, our memories of objects, people and events may be biassed. In general, frequently occurring events are usually recalled better and more quickly than less frequent events, which helps to overcome bias. However, this is not always the case. A situation in which the nature of the stimulus overcame frequency is illustrated by a group of people who were read a list of well known personalities. They were subsequently asked to judge whether the list contained more names of men or women. The subjects erroneously judged that the lists contained more men when in fact it had more *famous*, but less numerous, men than women, and vice versa.[18]

An example which you can try yourself is to assess whether there are more three-lettered words beginning with r than there are words with r as the third letter. Because it is easier to search our memory for words by their first letter than by their third letter, we usually judge that there are more words that begin with r whereas in reality there are more words that have r as the third letter. In this case again, the availability of recalled instances has biassed judgement. It is not always easy to overcome such biasses in the judgemental process, but keeping good records and using appropriate decision aids, when important judgements are being made, will help.

THE PERCEPTION – JUDGEMENT CONTINUUM

In the previous sections we have been examining different aspects of perception and judgement. However, it is worth remembering that perception and judgement form a continuum. All perceptions involve a judgement about what something is and all judgements are based on information gained from past perceptions. Two studies illustrate this continuum particularly well.

The first is a famous study carried out by Asch[19] in which college students were asked to state which of three lines was the same length as a standard line. The three lines were sufficiently different in length that subjects on their own rarely made mistakes. However, Asch tested subjects in a group situation where the other group members were actually confederates of the experimenter, who were primed to pick the wrong line on key trials where the real subject spoke last. Under these circumstances, 37% of real subjects went along with the group decision on any one trial, and over a series of trials 75% of real subjects gave in at least once. From our point of view, it is interesting to note that those who yielded did so for three main reasons. A few yielded at the *perceptual* level. They convinced themselves that they actually saw the lines in the same way as the other group members. Others yielded at *judgemental* level. They perceived the line correctly, but convinced themselves that their perceptions were inaccurate, and that those of the majority were correct. Thirdly, some subjects yielded at the *action* level. They perceived the line correctly and knew that they had perceived the line correctly, but went along with the majority because they did not wish to appear different from, or inferior to, the majority.

In the other study[20], subjects (University students) were presented with a brief description of a 'working man':

works in a factory	intelligent
reads a newspaper	strong
goes to movies	active
average height	

The inclusion of the adjective 'intelligent' posed a problem for many of the assessors, in that it did not fit in well with their picture of a typical factory worker. This problem was solved in several different ways:

- *Denial* A minority of subjects (5 out of 43)* refused to recognize the factory worker's level of intelligence or minimized it by saying such things as, "He is intelligent, but not too much so, since he works in a factory". Others (5) accepted that he was intelligent but denied he was a factory worker, in the sense that they promoted him to foreman.

- *Distortion* One of the most frequent ways (14 subjects) of reacting to the worker's intelligence was to modify the attribute in some way, either by reinterpreting it or by wrapping it up with another attribute so that it no longer conflicted with the assessors preconceived ideas. For example, it might be suggested that, although intelligent, the worker lacked the drive and initiative to rise above his group, or that he was not able to make use of his intelligence due to lack of formal education.

- *Change of Perception* Many subjects (14) were able to change their perception of the worker to incorporate the idea of him being intelligent. For example, he was seen as being witty and having a pleasant sense of humour rather than simply cracking jokes, and having a lively interest in the world around him rather than simply trying to keep up with what is going on. Even so, the worker's intelligence was seen only as affecting his interpersonal relations at work, not the way he performed the job itself.

- *Explicit Recognition of Incongruity* A small minority of subjects (3) recognized the disparity between their perception of a factory worker and the fact that he was described as intelligent, without actually changing

*The numbers quoted here do not total 43 because 5 subjects did not fit into any of the categories and others fell into more than one.

their perception of him. One, for example, stated, "the traits seem conflicting . . . most factory workers I have heard about aren't too intelligent".

In many respects, the latter response could be a highly adaptive one. The subject does have preconceived ideas about factory workers which are undoubtedly incorrect in many cases. Nevertheless, preconceived ideas are impossible to avoid. Life would be impossibly complicated if we had to keep an open mind on every single perception of a person or event. Furthermore, many of our preconceived ideas, e.g. 'boiling water scalds', 'fast moving cars hurt if they hit you', are not only correct, but dangerous to check. Where, however, something is perceived as conflicting with a preconceived idea, this can be a first step towards gathering further information which may result in the idea being changed or at least exceptions being recognized. We will take up this question again in a later section.

THE LEADER AS THE OBJECT OF PERCEPTION

So far we have been examining factors which affect the leader's ability to perceive people and events accurately. However, it must be remembered that leaders are themselves perceived by their followers. Furthermore, other people's perceptions of leaders are subject to the same sources of distortion we have already discussed. This is particularly so, if the information received from the leader is presented at a lower level of intensity, or is briefly expressed or is ambiguous in some way. Under these circumstances, the information may not be perceived at all or it may be distorted in the direction of the followers' expectations or self interest.

The apparent implication of this is that leaders should give information, orders, requests and so on in a clear, concise and unambiguous manner. Unfortunately, the situation is complicated by differences in perceptual ability among followers. One follower may be able to recognize and willing to act upon low level cues, and resent having everything spelled out in detail. Another may need to be told things very clearly in words of one syllable before one can be sure that there is little possibility of misinterpretation. Thus to communicate effectively, managers need to be aware of differences in perceptual ability amongst their subordinates (and others), and vary the explicitness or salience of their messages accordingly. If the message is particularly important, then it would be useful to check whether it has been interpreted correctly. In some cases, it may be sufficient simply to ask whether the person concerned understands, but it must be remembered that people will often say yes to avoid appearing stupid or annoying an authority figure. This in turn requires a close watch for nonverbal cues of doubt or rejection indicating that the message has not been understood or accepted. In addition, the manager can check whether the message has been correctly interpreted by getting the other person to restate it. For example: "Just to make sure we both understand what has come out of this discussion, perhaps you could summarize what has been agreed so far.'' This also has the advantage of helping the other person to remember what has been agreed, and making an overt statement of agreement may also act to increase the person's commitment to it.

A further perceptual problem may arise where the manager uses different styles of communication with the same subordinate under different circumstances. A simple example might be the army sergeant who insists on being referred to as 'sergeant' when officers are present, but prefers to be on first name terms with subordinates when they are not. Since subordinates will vary in their ability to recognize when a different managerial approach is being used, more explicit cues will sometimes be needed, e.g., ''This is an emergency. There is no time for discussion. This is what we are going to do'', or ''This is not a formal meeting. I simply want to get your views on the subject, so feel free to make any suggestions you wish''. Once having made such remarks, however, the manager must be very careful to control his or her own nonverbal cues. Subordinates are often very perceptive with respect to such things as half smiles and slight frowns, and may simply tell the boss what they think he or she wants to hear. This, and other matters discussed in this section will be examined in more detail in Chapter 5.

SUMMARY AND CONCLUSIONS

In this chapter we have shown that perception is not always as reliable as we might think. The old saying ''seeing is believing'' is certainly correct in that people tend to believe what they see. Unfortunately what they see—or hear—is not always what is there. Perception is inevitably selective. We cannot possibly attend to all the environmental stimuli which continually bombard us. Those we do perceive depend partly on the stimuli themselves, and partly on our needs and expectations. These factors not only determine *whether* we perceive something, but also *how* we perceive it. With ambiguous stimuli, our perceptions tend to be distorted in the direction of our needs and expectations. We tend to perceive what we want to perceive and what we expect to perceive.

Furthermore, research on eyewitness testimony[21] reveals an interesting fact. Certainty does not necessarily indicate accuracy. The eyewitness who says that he or she saw something ''without a shadow of a doubt'' may give no more accurate an account of what actually happened than one who says ''I think so, but I couldn't be sure''. Of course, we are all well aware that other people are very susceptible to this kind of thing. Most of us, no doubt, can recall examples of people who were totally sure of something, but also totally wrong. However, we seem less able to recognize that we might ourselves be wrong when we are convinced about something. Yet, if pressed, few of us would claim to be the only person in the world completely unsusceptible to errors of perception. So it may be worthwhile to bear in mind that it could happen to us, and perhaps occasionally remind ourselves that it could be happening right now!

In that case, what can be done to minimize the likelihood of misperception? We would suggest the following:

- Do not assume that just because you have seen or heard something, it is categorically true.
- Be doubly cautious about accepting second-hand information at face value. The more people there are involved in transmitting the information, the greater the opportunities for omission and distortion.
- Treat perceptions as hypothesis, to be checked out by collecting further information.
- Be on the look out for contradictory evidence, particularly when interacting with other people. Do not answer your own questions. Let the other person answer, and *listen* to the answer they give, watching out particularly for nonverbal cues to the emotional content of their response.
- Do not project your own feelings and emotions on to other people.
- Do not assume that history always repeats itself. Just because one representative of a group (race, social class, sex, etc.) behaves or reacts in a certain way, does not mean that the next one will. Note also that people change over time too. Just because that is what a subordinate wanted in the past, does not mean that he or she wants it now.
- Check your own motives when making decisions. They may have unconsciously influenced the way you saw the situation and the conclusions reached.

NOTES AND REFERENCES

1   It is worth noting that this process starts immediately something is perceived, otherwise all we would see or hear would be a meaningless jumble of sense data. On the other hand, we may also consciously attempt to puzzle out the precise implications of some unclear information we perceived some time previously. Thus, although we have presented perception and judgement as separate processes for the sake of convenience, and because judgement does sometimes occur on its own, the two processes are largely merged in practice.

2   See for example: MD Storms (1973), 'Videotape and the Attribution Process: Reversing Actors' and Observers' Point of View', *Journal of Personality and Social Psychology*, Vol. 27, pp. 165–175; and SE Taylor and ST Fiske (1978), 'Salience, Attention and Attribution: Top of the Head Phenomena', in L Berkowitz (ed.), *Advances in Experimental Social Psychology*, Vol. 11, Academic Press.

3   R Buckhout (1974), 'Eyewitness Testimony', *Scientific American*. Vol. 231, No. 6, pp. 23–31.

4   DL Rosenhan (1973), 'On Being Sane in Insane Places', *Science, NY*, Vol. 179, pp. 250–258.

5   A Anastasi (1964), *Fields of Occupational Psychology*, McGraw-Hill, p. 96.

6   BM Springbett (1958), 'Factors Affecting the Final Decision in the Employment Interview', *Canadian Journal of Psychology*, Vol. 12, pp. 13–22.

7   FJ Landy, RJ Vance, JL Barnes-Farrell and JW Steele (1980), 'Statistical Control of Halo Error in Performance Ratings', *Journal of Applied Psychology*, Vol. 65, pp. 501–506.

8 KK Dion, E Berscheid and E Walster (1972), 'What is Beautiful is Good', *Journal of Personality and Social Psychology*, Vol. 24, pp. 285–290.

9 RD Arvey (1979), 'Unfair Discrimination in the Employment Interview: Legal and Psychological Aspects', *Psychological Bulletin*, Vol. 86, pp. 736–765.

10 K Simas and M McCarrey (1979), 'Impact of Recruiter Authoritarianism and Applicant Sex on Evaluation and Selection Decisions in a Recruitment Interview Analogue Study', *Journal of Applied Psychology*, Vol. 64, pp. 483–491.

11 JR Terborg and DR Ilgen (1975), 'A Theoretical Approach to Sex Discrimination in Traditionally Masculine Occupations', *Organisational Behaviour and Human Performance*, Vol. 13, pp. 352–376.

12 R Likert (1961), *New Patterns of Management*, McGraw-Hill, p. 91.

13 S Lieberman (1956), 'The Effects of Changes in Roles on the Attitudes of Role Occupants', *Human Relations*, Vol. 9, pp. 385–402.

14 DC Dearborn and HA Simon (1958), 'Selective Perception: A Note on the Departmental Identification of Executives', *Sociometry*, Vol. 21, pp. 140–144.

15 TW Costello and SS Zalkind (1963), *Psychology in Administration: A Research Orientation*, Prentice-Hall, pp. 135–136.

16 F Sanford (1965), *Psychology: A Scientific Study of Man*, Wadsworth, p. 466.

17 Costello and Zalkind (1963), *op. cit.*, pp. 148–149.

18 A Tversky and D Kahneman (1973), 'A Heuristic for Judging Frequency and Probability', *Cognitive Psychology*, Vol. 5, pp. 207–232.

19 SE Asch (1956), 'Studies of Independence and Conformity. I: A Minority of One Against a Unanimous Majority', *Psychological Monographs: General and Applied*, Vol. 70, No. 9, pp. 1–70.

20 M Haire and WF Grunes (1950), 'Perceptual Defenses: Processes Protecting an Organized Perception of Another Person', *Human Relations*, Vol. 3, pp. 403–412.

21 KA Deffenbacher (1980), 'Eyewitness Accuracy and Confidence: Can We Infer Anything about their Relationship', *Law and Human Behavior*, Vol. 4, pp. 243–260.

Chapter 4

Verbal Components of Manager–Subordinate Interactions

INTRODUCTION

In this chapter, we come to what we consider to be the most important aspect of the interpersonal skills of leadership—what managers actually say and do when interacting with their subordinates. Undoubtedly, many other factors contribute to successful leadership. The manager may already have carried out a detailed analysis of the factors influencing the subordinate's performance, and also have cleared his or her mind of any preconceptions which could lead to distortions of perception or judgement. The manager may also have decided how to structure the interaction—which topics are to be dealt with and in what order—and decided on his or her general approach to the subordinate—friendly, considerate, stern, unyielding and so on. Nevertheless, this still leaves the manager with the problem of what he or she is to say to the subordinate and how to say it. Throughout the interaction, the manager must decide what to say or do *next* in order to achieve his or her objectives. As we noted in Chapter 1, this is an aspect of leadership on which the practising manager will receive remarkably little help from leadership theories. Yet it is crucial. If it is mishandled—if the manager says the wrong thing, or says it in the wrong way—then the interaction may fail, no matter how careful the manager's preparations or how good his or her intentions.

In our view, what is required as a first step towards helping managers to develop this aspect of leadership skills is a checklist of the various things which *could* be said and done in interactions with their subordinates, and guidelines which will help them to select those which would be most appropriate for a particular purpose. We would suggest that the manager's behaviour in interactions with his or her subordinates can usefully be regarded as being made up of a number of primary components. These are the basic building blocks out of which the manager's contribution to the interaction as a whole is constructed. Such components may be verbal or nonverbal. Verbal components include the various questions and statements employed by the manager during the interaction. These will be discussed in the present chapter. Nonverbal components, which we will examine in Chapter 5, consist of such things as tone of voice, gestures, body posture, facial expressions, and so on, which accompany speech and sometimes replace it. To rephrase the statement at the beginning of this paragraph, then, our aim in these two chapters is to provide checklists of the various verbal and nonverbal components which are available to managers in interactions with their subordinates, and guidelines which will help them to select those components which are the most appropriate for the particular purpose at hand.

Apart from idle conversation, there are three main purposes which a manager may wish to pursue in an interaction with a subordinate. These are gathering information, influencing behaviour, and handling emotion. In some cases, the manager may be primarily concerned with achieving only one of these objectives. For example, in one interaction, the manager's main aim may be to discover the subordinate's opinion concerning a particular piece of equipment before deciding whether a repeat order should be placed. In another, the manager's prime concern may be to let the subordinate know that an improvement in work performance is necessary in some particular area. In a third, the manager may simply wish to listen sympathetically thus allowing a subordinate to get a grievance or personal problem off his or her chest. Often, however, it will be necessary to fulfil all three objectives during the same interaction. If the manager does not simply wish to act as a 'sounding board', but actually wants to help the subordinate towards a solution to the problem, then further information will be required and perhaps also a change in the behaviour of the subordinate. Similarly, deciding precisely how someone should improve his or her performance may also require additional information, and the attempt to get someone to change his or her work behaviour may lead to adverse emotional reactions. The interpersonally skilled manager must be able to perform each of these activities well. Let us examine each in turn.

GATHERING INFORMATION

The ability to obtain precise, valid and relevant information from people is an extremely useful aspect of a manager's repertoire of skills. It can be used in a wide variety of managerial situations, for example, selection interviewing, identifying customer needs, pinning down suppliers on precise specifications or delivery dates, obtaining information from one's own boss or fellow managers and so on. It is also an extremely important aspect of modern leadership skills.

An important source of information are the subordinates themselves. They may be able to provide information which will help the manager to do his or her own job more efficiently. They will almost certainly be able to identify factors which influence their own performance, either beneficially or adversely. Furthermore, they may be able to suggest changes which can be made which would enable them to improve their work performance. This does not mean that such information will invariably be totally accurate. Like anyone else, subordinates may misunderstand the real factors influencing their performance, or may consciously or unconsciously distort the information in the direction of their own self interest. However, this does not render the information valueless. Rather it means that more skilful questionning is required, despite the possibility of misunderstanding or distortion on the part of the subordinate.

The questions and statements used to gather information can conveniently be grouped under three headings. Firstly, there are those which are explicitly concerned with *eliciting information*. In different ways, they all ask the subordinate to provide information on a particular topic, however broadly or narrowly defined. Included here are the following:

Open Questions These ask for general information concerning some topic area. For example:

"What do you think of the new stamping machine?"

"Tell me what steps you have taken to deal with the absenteeism problem."

"How do you see your career developing in the immediate future?"

By asking the question in this form, the manager allows the subordinate to decide what information he or she thinks is relevant within some general area. They are also couched in such a way that a simple yes or no is not appropriate. Thus open questions are useful for encouraging a subordinate to talk about a particular topic area at some length, expressing his or her own thoughts, when the manager does not have a clear idea of the specific information he or she requires. Thus, at the very least, open questions should provide useful background information concerning a particular topic. They may also elicit the more specific information the manager requires, either by chance or because the subordinate is perceptive and realizes what the manager is looking for. If they do not, however, a different kind of question is needed.

Probes Probing questions are useful for obtaining more detailed information and opinions. For example:

"What particular complaints have the operators made about the new stamping machine?"

"What is the most serious problem you have to deal with when absenteeism goes over 10%"

"What is it that particularly attracts you to that kind of work?"

Such questions often follow open questions, and are used to pin down something described in more general terms in response to the open question. However, care must be taken not to employ too threatening a manner particularly when probing sensitive areas, as the interaction could take on the attributes of a 'third degree' and arouse resistance and resentment.

Closed Questions These are useful for establishing specific points of fact, e.g. simple yes or no answers, numbers, dates. Examples include:

"What is the delivery date for the replacement stamping machine?"

"How many days were lost last month due to absence?"

"Would you be interested in a secondment to Product Development for three months?"

Obviously, if the manager wishes to obtain such specific pieces of information, and the subordinate is ready to supply them, there is little reason to talk round the subject by asking open questions. Conversely, however, they are much less useful for obtaining general background information, particularly with relatively taciturn subordinates who may simply give such answers as "March 26th", "114" or "Yes". Thus attempts to gather information employing a predominance of closed questions run the danger of being short and lacking in background information, additional details and personal opinions which might completely change the complexion of the information given. This can, of course, be blamed on the taciturn nature of the subordinate, but the fault lies equally with the manager for not asking the right sort of questions.

Comparisons These can be used to get the subordinate to explore facts in a new light or reveal his or her own needs, values and opinions. For example:

"What do you think are the relative merits of the current stamping machine and the new machine which will become available later this year?"

"Are there any major differences in patterns of absenteeism between employees who live locally and those who have to travel further?"

"Would you prefer to develop your career on the technical side or in line management?"

Obviously, the pairs chosen must be relevant and realistic, so that it is within the capability of the subordinate to make a considered judgement. Also, it may be useful to set the scene by explaining why the question is being asked, otherwise the subordinate may suspect an ulterior motive and be reluctant to give his or her true opinions (see 'Trap Setting' in Chapter 6).

Hypotheticals Hypothetical questions represent another way of encouraging the subordinate to explore his or her ideas or feelings about a particular subject. For example:

"If we were offered a replacement for the existing stamping machine, do you think we should take it?"

"Supposing absenteeism were to exceed your predictions for any reason, how would that affect your production forecasts?"

"How would you feel if you were offered a promotion which involved a move to a different part of the country?"

It must be stressed that the main aim of hypothetical questions should be to get the subordinate to consider new ideas, or allow the manager to assess the subordinate's depth of knowledge in a particular area or ability to come to reasoned conclusions about a particular problem. It should not be assumed that the answers necessarily represent what the subordinate would really do should the situation actually arise. After further thought, perhaps triggered by the question itself, the subordinate might later change his or her mind. If the outcome is important to the manager, therefore, a further check at some later date may be useful. Furthermore, as with comparisons, the hypothetical situation which is posed should be selected carefully and, where necessary, background information given. Otherwise, there is the danger that the subordinate may lack the knowledge or experience to come to a meaningful conclusion. Alternatively, the question may raise unrealistic expectations which cannot be fulfilled at a later date, causing resentment, or the subordinate may suspect a trap and refuse to fall into it. Hypotheticals often fail spectacularly if they are used in an attempt to make someone see another person's viewpoint or feel shame, perhaps because people have learned how to cope with them from early experience. For example:

Manager: "How would you feel if I reprimanded you like that?"

Subordinate: "I wouldn't make such a stupid mistake in the first place, so you wouldn't have to"

Manager: "But supposing you did, how would you feel?"

Subordinate: "I would think that I deserved to be reprimanded, and I would accept it"

Manager: "But wouldn't you feel resentful if you were reprimanded like that?"

Subordinate: "I might at first, but I would soon realize that it was entirely justified. Did you see what he did? He . . ."

This is rapidly turning into a win—lose interaction (see Chapter 7 for more detailed discussion of this problem). Someone is going to have to back down, either the subordinate by showing compliance, e.g. "OK I take your point" or the manager by changing the subject, with very little gained on either side. An alternative method of tackling such a problem (causal analysis) is discussed in Chapter 6.

Multiple Questions These are the only type of question amongst those listed which we regard as serving no useful purpose whatsoever. They consist of a string of questions linked together without pauses where the other person may respond. Sometimes they occur because the manager wishes to have answers to a number of related questions and cannot wait to ask them one at a time, and sometimes because the manager is not satisfied with the way he or she has expressed a particular question and therefore rephrases it in several different ways. The following is an example incorporating both aspects:

"Have you done anything to reduce the high rates of absenteeism in your section? How many days did you lose last month? Did you notice any significant patterns in the absenteeism data? I mean, were there any particular jobs which had higher absenteeism rates or any particular people who were off more than others? Did you check out how your section compares with the others in the department?"

It is very unlikely that the subordinate will be able to remember this string of questions and therefore answer all of them. Even if the subordinate could remember them, the answer might be "No, I've been too busy, 36, yes, no, yes, yes and they are worse", which would be of little use to the manager. Of course, what is much more likely is that the subordinate, consciously or unconsciously, will select the question in the list which is easiest, or least incriminating, to answer, and reply at length, hoping to lead the discussion on to less threatening topics. For example:

"Yes, there is one of the employees who has a particularly poor attendance record. That's Mrs Burns. Her daughter has been ill recently, and she says that there is no-one else who can take her to the hospital. I've talked to her several times about it, but from what I've heard, her daughter really is sick, so I don't feel I can lean on her too hard. What do you think I should do in a case like that?"

What makes things worse is that buried amongst the string of questions which the manager asked is often a particularly good one which would have produced relevant and useful information, but which is never answered as the discussion changes direction. Thus it is much better to ask a single question and listen to the answer before asking the next one. Even if it is less well expressed than the manager would like, the subordinate may still answer the question the manager meant to ask. If not, it is still possible to follow up with a more precise question after the subordinate has replied.

The second major group of information gathering components are those concerned with *managing the flow of information*. Included here are what we refer to as 'lubricators', 'inhibitors' and 'bridges'.

Lubricators These include such words, phrases and vocalizations as "Yes", "Go on", "I see", "mmm", "Uh huh", and so on. If accompanied by the appropriate nonverbal cues of interest (see p. 80), they encourage people to continue talking on a particular subject.

Inhibitors Examples of inhibitors are "I see", "Oh", "Yes, but" and so on which, if accompanied by nonverbal cues of disinterest (see p. 80) or signs that the manager wishes to take over the speaking role (see p. 82) indicate that the subordinate has said enough on a particular topic. Tone of voice is particularly important here. Thus a word or phrase, e.g. "Yes", could act as a lubricator if said slowly and relatively softly, or act as an inhibitor if said shortly, sharply and relatively loudly.

Both lubricators and inhibitors operate at a largely unconscious level. Unless the manager is very self aware, he or she probably does not realize that a subordinate is being encouraged to continue to speak or to abandon some topic by means of lubricators, inhibitors and their associated nonverbal signals. Similarly, the subordinate is unlikely to realize quite how much he or she responds to such signals. Most people, in fact, seem to use such cues effectively most of the time, without thinking about it. However, there are occasions when problems can arise. Some people habitually do not display signs of interest or emotion very clearly, and are therefore very difficult to 'read'. Thus lack of lubricators could be mistakenly interpreted as lack of interest. In other cases, the use of lubricators or inhibitors could be inconsistent with other aspects of the manager's behaviour, perhaps due to a conflict of motives. For example, a manager may use an open question because he or she thinks the subordinate should be encouraged to talk, and then follow this up with inhibitors, or at least an absence of lubricators, because the manager isn't really interested in what the subordinate has to say. The manager may then blame the subordinate's short and incomplete replies on the fact that the latter "isn't very forthcoming" rather than his or her own questionning technique.

Bridges In longer interactions, bridges provide a smooth transition between one topic and the next. For example:

> "Well, I think that we have got as far as we can with the absenteeism problem for the time being. Let's turn to another topic which I think we need to discuss. I've been wondering whether we should replace the stamping machine. What do you think . . ."

This is perhaps not the most important component in the manager's repertoire of interpersonal skills. Nevertheless, it does signal to subordinates that a new topic is being introduced and give them an opportunity to collect their thoughts on it, and it does add a certain amount of elegance to the discussion.

The final group of information gathering components are those involved in *checking agreement concerning actions and events.* Included here are restatements and summaries.

Restatements These involve restating or paraphrasing the subordinate's comments. Said in a slightly questionning, but nevertheless accepting tone of voice, their aim is to allow managers to check on the accuracy of their perception of what the subordinate has just said or to get the subordinate to crystallize ideas which have not been clearly expressed. For example:

> "What you seem to be telling me is that the machine is ideal for routine work, but cannot easily be reset for one-off jobs".

This not only ensures that the manager has not misunderstood the subordinate's comments, but also allows time to think about how to proceed with the issue in question. However, care must again be taken with accompanying nonverbal cues. Said in the wrong tone of voice or with the wrong facial expression, such restatements could indicate rejection, surprise, ridicule, disgust, etc. Alternatively, if said with force and conviction, they could lead a compliant subordinate to agree, even though the restatement did not accurately reflect their views (see leading questions in the next section).

Summaries These draw together the main points of a discussion. They can be used at the end of an interaction to draw together all the major points discussed or, in the longer interactions, they may be used at the end of a particular section of the discussion before proceeding to the next. For example:

> "What we have agreed so far, then, is that you will provide a breakdown of absenteeism figures by individual employees, type of work, day of the week, and so on, over the next month, and see whether any patterns emerge. We will then go through this data together at our next meeting and see what steps can be taken to solve the problem. In the meantime, I will talk to Personnel to see whether they have any useful suggestions, or at least will be willing to back us

if we do try to do something, and you will have a word with some of the persistent offenders to see whether there are any particular problems we should know about. OK?''

The advantage of an interim summary is that it ensures that there is agreement before going on to the next issue, thus reducing the likelihood that manager and subordinate will be at cross purposes during the subsequent discussion. It also makes it much easier to carry out a final summary, because the main conclusions have already been agreed at strategic points throughout the discussion. Final summaries serve several useful functions. They reduce the liklihood of subsequent differences of opinion between manager and subordinate concerning the main outcomes of the discussion. In longer discussions, they serve to remind participants of points made earlier which might otherwise have been forgotten. Given that there is a tendency for memory as well as perception to be selective, it is sometimes useful to ask the subordinate to do the summary. This will enable the manager to check on whether the subordinate has in fact remembered the main points of the discussion accurately or at all. Finally, summarizing and gaining agreement to do something can also help in gaining the subordinate's commitment to put into action any specific plans which emerged from the discussion. This last point brings us to the second major group of verbal components—those concerned with influencing behaviour.

The various types of question and statement described in this section are summarized in Table 2, together with an indication of the situations in which their use would be appropriate or inappropriate.

INFLUENCING BEHAVIOUR

Although the primary purpose of the question and statement types we have just described is to gather information, under certain circumstances it is also possible to use them as a means of influencing behaviour. With able and experienced subordinates, such information gathering techniques can be used to stimulate them to analyze their own performance problems or development needs and formulate their own solutions or personal development plans. This requires the skilful use of open questions, probes, hypotheticals, restatements, and so on to guide the subordinate to restructure or reorganize problems so that new ways of tackling them can be explored. A short example of this approach is given in Chapter 6 (see 'Causal Analysis'). Indeed previous lists of question and statement types, such as those of Randell[1] and Zima,[2] have concentrated entirely on those involved in gathering information or handling emotion.

The advantages of this approach are broadly twofold. Firstly, it is likely to develop high levels of commitment to the solutions reached because they are largely the subordinate's own solutions. Secondly, it is likely to improve the subordinate's problem solving ability because the manager is, in effect, coaching the subordinate in methods of analyzing and solving performance problems. Nevertheless, such a nondirective approach is not always appropriate

Table 2 Components for Gathering Information

(a) Components for Eliciting Information from the Subordinate

Component	Appropriate use	Inappropriate use
Open questions e.g. "Tell me about . . ." "Could you describe what you think are . . ."	For introducing topics and encouraging subordinates to talk at length so avoiding simple yes and no answers	For obtaining specific details
Probes e.g. "Could you tell me more about . . .?" "What do you mean by . . .?"	Generally follow open questions to elicit more information about a particular topic or event	For exploring emotionally charged areas
Closed questions e.g. "How long did it take?" "Did you receive my draft report?"	Establishing precise information and receiving simple yes and no responses	For gaining broad information, opinions, etc.
Comparisons e.g. "What are the relative merits of . . .?"	Getting subordinates to explore and reveal their own needs, values and opinions	Where the 'pairs' are unrealistic or irrelevant
Hypotheticals e.g. "What would you do (have done) about (if) . . .?"	Getting subordinates to think about a new topic or area	When a subordinate lacks knowledge or experience of the situation described
Multiples A stream of questions or statements strung together covering several points	None. The respondent usually answers the last question or the one most convenient for him to answer	Always inappropriate

(b) Components for Managing the Flow of Information

Component	Appropriate use	Inappropriate use
Lubricators e.g. "Ye-es" "Go on', "mmm", "Ah ha"	Indicating to sub-ordinates that you are listening and want them to continue	With over-talkative sub-ordinates. Over-used they become intrusive and inhibiting
Inhibitors e.g. "Oh!", "I see", "Yes but"	Signalling that enough has been said. N.B. tone of voice may indicate surprise, indignation or non-acceptance of views expressed	With reticent sub-ordinates. For frank and open discussion. Where frustration or emotion is being expressed
Bridges e.g. "I think that's all we need to say on that topic, now let's turn to . . ."	Providing a smooth link between one topic and another and indicating clearly what the next one is	When the previous topic has not been adequately dealt with from the subordinate's point of view

(c) Checking Agreement Concerning Actions and Events

Restatements e.g. "What you seem to be telling me is that . . ."	To confirm or crystallize ideas	When used dispar-agingly or reproach-fully, sarcastically or cynically
Summaries e.g. "What we seem to have discussed and decided so far is . . ."	Drawing together the main points of a discussion and avoiding discrepancies. It can also help in gaining commitment to action	If used prematurely

for several reasons. It can be time consuming. Subordinates may lack the ability or experience to identify solutions to their own performance problems. Finally, the manager may have learned from past experience that the subordinate is likely to produce solutions which are impractical or irrelevant and become annoyed if they are not accepted. In some situations, therefore, more directive methods of influencing behaviour are called for, and it is necessary for the manager to spell out in detail what behaviour is expected from the subordinate. It is these more directive methods of influencing behaviour which we will be examining in the remainder of this section.

Behavioural influence components do not fall neatly into distinct categories, as do those for gathering information. Nevertheless, two main aspects can be identified—*direction* and *inducement*. Components which give direction tell the subordinate what the manager wants or expects him or her to do. Inducements, on the other hand, are components which are intended to persuade the subordinate to do it. Some components, as we shall see later, can fulfil both functions if used skilfully.

Components which provide direction include orders, requests, advice and suggestions. These vary in the extent to which the manager indicates that the subordinate is obliged to follow the manager's wishes.

Orders These give the subordinate least room for manoeuvre. They indicate that the manager expects his or her wishes to be carried out without question. No participation in the decision is invited. Thus subordinates cannot express their own opinions or preferences without running the risk of overt conflict. For example:

> "In future you will not order replacement parts for the stamping machine without first consulting me, and then only if I give you permission in writing."

Requests Like orders, requests indicate the manager's wishes, but, in theory at least, give the subordinate the right to refuse, express reservations, or suggest alternatives. For example:

> "In future I would appreciate it if you would consult me before ordering replacement parts for the stamping machine and preferably obtain my permission in writing."

Advice/Suggestions These are similar to requests, but imply that the subordinate should comply because it would be in the subordinate's own interests or it would be organizationally more effective, rather than simply because the manager says so. Thus they stress the authority relationship between manager and subordinate much less than orders or requests. For example:

> "In future why don't you come and discuss the matter with me beforehand and get my signature on any requests for spare parts for the stamping machine? I think you would find that things would go a lot more smoothly if you did."

Which particular component is the most appropriate in any one situation will depend on a variety of factors. These include the organizational climate, the power of the manager, the preferences of the subordinate, and the severity of the consequences of noncompliance on the part of the subordinate. In some organizations, giving orders is an accepted way of influencing behaviour, whereas in others it would be regarded as inappropriate. Even within the same organization, subordinates are likely to vary in their preferences with respect to the way in which their managers make their wishes known to them. Some may prefer clear cut orders which leave the responsibility for the decision squarely in the manager's hands. Others may respond with enthusiasm to a mild suggestion, but would resent being ordered to do something, and do it with much less commitment. The organizational power of the manager is important in that it determines the extent to which the manager can enforce compliance with his or her wishes should the subordinate refuse or fail to obey a direct order. If the subordinate is likely to refuse an order and can do so with impunity, then more persuasive methods may be more appropriate. Finally, much will depend upon how strongly the manager feels that noncompliance on the part of the subordinate would have serious organizational consequences. If the consequences are likely to be very serious, e.g. a strike, major loss of business, a serious accident, the manager may feel that he or she cannot risk noncompliance and issue a direct order. Similarly, if the subordinate has not responded to requests, advice, or suggestions in the past, with adverse consequences, then the manager may decide that it is better to 'lay it on the line', rather than risk a repetition. On the other hand, if the consequences of noncompliance are unlikely to be severe, the manager may well think it worthwhile to use a milder request or suggestion because this would increase the subordinate's self esteem, positive feelings towards his or her boss, enthusiasm for the task, and so on.

Ultimately, then, the component selected should be the one which is most likely to ensure that the manager's wishes are carried out with commitment. All this assumes, of course, that the manager is in full possession of all the facts and is sure that his or her decision is the right one in the first place. If not, and time is available, then it may be that an information gathering approach would be more appropriate.

The components so far discussed simply let the subordinate know what the manager's wishes are. Inducements, on the other hand, give the subordinate reasons, either personal or organizational, for complying with such wishes. These include promises, threats and explanations.

Promises These indicate that compliance with the manager's wishes will have beneficial outcomes for the subordinate. For example:

"And on my part, I will put pressure on Purchasing Department to do all they can to speed up delivery on essential replacement orders."
"We will look at the situation again in six months time, and if it isn't working as smoothly as we would like, then we will reconsider our current procedures."

One way in which promises can vary is in the extent to which their fulfilment is made contingent on performance. If the promise is without strings and requires no further action on the part of the subordinate, it may serve to increase his or her level of job satisfaction, reduce any feelings of resentment or frustration, and engender a more favourable attitude towards the boss. This in turn may result in the subordinate being in a more receptive frame of mind for the rest of the discussion. Where the promise concerns the removal of some factor which is impeding the subordinate's work performance, it may also increase the subordinate's enthusiasm for the task. However, there is little evidence that improving job satisfaction will in itself lead to improved job performance. If the manager wishes to use promises to motivate the subordinate to improve his or her job performance, therefore, fulfilment of such promises must be made contingent on the subordinate achieving the desired improvement. Thus they are useful in situations where subordinates cannot see a clear link between their performance and the extrinsic rewards they receive, or where they do not regard existing rewards as being sufficient to merit the effort required to achieve them.

Used in this way, promises can provide a useful way of motivating subordinates to whom extrinsic rewards are important. They have the advantage over threats that subordinates are more likely to work with enthusiasm and commitment towards the achievement of a desirable goal than the avoidance of an unpleasant outcome. Also, if the rewards promised are both equitable and achievable, the subordinates are more likely to develop favourable attitudes towards their jobs, the manager and the organization as a whole.

Nevertheless, promises can have disadvantages as means of influencing behaviour. They can become addictive. If the manager always promises something, and fulfils the promise, whenever the subordinate shows reluctance to do something, then the manager is, in effect, rewarding the subordinate for showing reluctance. This could lead to a situation where the subordinate shows reluctance with increasing regularity and the manager rapidly runs out of things to promise. Care should be taken therefore to ensure that what is promised is a legitimate and equitable reward for the performance in question.

Threats These indicate that failure to comply with the manager's wishes will have adverse consequences as far as the subordinate is concerned. For example:
> "If there are any further incidents of this type, I shall have no alternative but to express strong reservations about your current performance and future career prospects in your annual report. Furthermore, I will instruct Purchasing Department not to accept any of your orders unless countersigned by me personally."

As we have already indicated, the use of threats clearly has disadvantages in that they may reduce the subordinate's enthusiasm for his or her job and cause resentment towards the manager or the organization as a whole. Nevertheless, they still represent a useful and legitimate means of influencing behaviour under certain circumstances. If the subordinate's work performance is clearly inadequate in some respect, and other methods of behavioural influence have failed, then threats may represent the only alternative to doing nothing, and the manager who simply ignored a subordinate's inadequate performance would also be failing in his or her own job. Furthermore, in many cases doing nothing is unfair to the subordinate. Inadequate job performance often has its own adverse consequences, such as being overlooked for promotion, poor salary increases, lower bonuses, and even the ultimate sanction of dismissal. It is much better to let the subordinate know that such consequences may occur if performance is not improved than to apply them later, when it is too late for the subordinate to do anything to remedy the situation.

In the case of both promises and threats, what is promised or threatened is extremely important. They must involve outcomes which matter to the subordinate and they must be pitched at the right level. With respect to promises, the manager must identify precisely what the subordinate would like to have *next* which would be sufficient to motivate the desired behaviour and which is within the manager's power to grant. This means that the manager must have a good understanding of what motivates the subordinate in question. To offer something which does not interest the subordinate will obviously not have the desired effect. Similarly, offering a subordinate less than he or she thinks is worthwhile in terms of the effort involved is likely to be ineffective, and the subordinate may resent the implication that he or she can be 'bought' so cheaply. Conversely, offering the subordinate significantly more than would be necessary to motivate the desired change in behaviour could represent a waste of organizational resources and will reduce the range of things which the manager can offer for an improvement in performance next time.

Similar considerations apply with respect to threats. The outcome threatened must be something which the subordinate would prefer to avoid, and the consequences sufficiently severe to motivate the desired change in behaviour. Again, however, threatening an outcome more severe than would be necessary to produce the desired behaviour change would be counter productive. Not only is this likely to cause unnecessary resentment, but it could actually have an adverse effect on performance rather than improve it. High levels of anxiety, particularly on complex tasks may make the person too tense to be able to perform well. Furthermore, research into attitude change suggests that high levels of fear may produce less attitude change than moderate or low levels. It seems that people subjected to high levels of fear arousal find this so aversive that they tend to ignore or minimize the importance of the threat.[3] However, there is also evidence that whatever the level of fear arousal, it is much more likely to lead to a change in attitudes and behaviour if the fear arousal is accompanied by specific recommendations concerning the actions which should be taken to avoid the threatened consequences.[4] Thus, if used, threats should be accompanied by directive components spelling out in detail what the subordinate needs to do in order to avoid the threat being fulfilled.

It is also important, when using promises or threats, that the manager is both willing and able to carry them out. There is little point in describing the most attractive or aversive outcomes if the subordinate knows from past experience that neither is likely to be fulfilled.

Explanations Used as an inducement, explanations tell the subordinate why he or she should or should not take certain actions because of their effect on organizational performance, other people within the organization, or even the subordinate in question. In other words, they are concerned with the 'logic of the situation' rather than any subsequent actions the manager might take to reward or punish the subordinate in question. For example:

> "We need to coordinate the ordering of replacement parts on a departmental basis. If everyone ordered parts independently, it could lead to unnecessary duplication, and the loss of any economies which could be made through bulk purchase. And of course, it could lead to considerable resentment on the part of your colleagues if you were allowed to bypass the formal system and they were not. Not to mention the fact that I could look very stupid if my boss asked me why we were making one-off replacement orders, and I didn't even know anything about it."

Explanations can provide an effective way of influencing behaviour. Many people respond much more willingly to an attempt to get them to do something, or to change what they are doing, if it is explained why it is necessary for them to do so. It can add to intrinsic motivation by making the task more meaningful. It can also add to, or at least not detract from, their self esteem, because they are being treated as thinking human beings with a need to understand what they are doing. Nevertheless, explanations may not always produce the desired motivation to change. The subordinate may disagree with the manager's assessment of the situation and the organizational consequences of his or her current way of doing things. Alternatively, the subordinate may be more concerned with the effect of any changes on his or her own self interest than with their effect on the organization or other people. Such self interest may not, of course, emerge overtly in the discussion. It may instead, consciously or unconsciously, distort the subordinate's assessment of the situation and its organizational consequences. Equally, it is possible that the manager's initial assessment of the situation, was distorted in much the same way. Thus there may ensue a long, counterproductive difference of opinion in which the real issues are never discussed. Unless the manager is sure that his or her assessment of the situation is unbiassed, therefore, other methods of influencing behaviour (promises, threats, a straightforward order without explanation) may be more appropriate.

Inducement and directive components are, of course, often used in conjunction with each other. It is possible to use a directive component, such as an order or request, without adding an explicit inducement, relying on the manager's implicit reward and punishment power or the subordinate's trust in the manager's judgement of fairness to ensure compliance. Similarly, it is possible to use inducement, such as threats or promises to influence a subordinate's general emotional state by issuing them without conditions or any indication of how the threatened outcome can be avoided. On the other hand, if such inducements are used in an attempt to influence a specific aspect of performance, then it is necessary to spell out the behaviour required, which in turn requires the use of directive components. Thus for example, an order, request, suggestion, or advice not to wedge fire doors open whilst transferring files from one office to another might be combined with such inducements as:

". . . because a fire would spread more quickly if they are wedged open." (explanation)

". . . because I will institute formal disciplinary proceedings if you do." (threat)

". . . and I will look into alternative methods of transporting the files." (promise)

One of the ways in which both direction and inducement can vary is in their precision. "Keep up the good work and I will see that you are all right" includes elements of both direction and inducement, but neither is very clearly spelled out. "Keep up the good work and I will put you up for promotion in the next staff review" provides a very specific inducement combined with vague direction. Conversely, "If you wedge those fire doors open again, I will not be responsible for the consequences" combines a very precise direction with a rather vague inducement.

One of the more subtle skills of leadership is achieving the appropriate degree of precision with which both aspects are spelled out. Going over the details of a task which the subordinate already understands or giving someone precise orders to do something which he or she was going to do anyway is likely to be at best irritating and at worst highly demotivating (see 'Hammering the Point Home', Chapter 6). Similarly, giving staff precise inducements for doing something they already find intrinsically motivating may, in some circumstances, actually decrease the level of intrinsic motivation. Conversely, if directions and inducements are not spelled out clearly enough, subordinates may not know what it is the manager wishes them to do or may not understand the consequences clearly enough to be motivated to do it. The situation is further complicated by the facts that subordinates will differ in the speed with which they grasp the implications of what the manager is saying, and that the same subordinate could grasp things very quickly on one occasion, but take much longer to understand an apparently simple point on another. This could be highly misleading if the manager has preconceived ideas about the subordinate's speed of comprehension, and fails to notice that the subordinate is not reacting as quickly—or as slowly—as the manager has grown to expect. Furthermore, verbal agreement or acquiescence is not necessarily a sign of comprehension or commitment. The subordinate may not wish to appear stupid or may wish to avoid further criticism. One of the quickest ways to terminate the discussion is to agree. Thus, a comment such as: "OK, I take your point. I'll make sure it doesn't happen again" may simply be a means of escaping from an unpleasant situation. It is all too easy to say "Good, I'm glad you got the message". However, a follow-up probing question, such as "What exactly would you do differently if the same situation arose again?'' might reveal that the subordinate had not fully understood the problem.

Thus, hard and fast rules cannot be given. It is a question of spelling out directions and inducements in sufficient detail to ensure the change in behaviour which is desired, but not going beyond this and labouring the point. Observational skills are, therefore, particularly important. The manager must actively listen and look for the various verbal and nonverbal signs of understanding or confusion, acceptance or rejection, interest or irritation, commitment or mere compliance, and be prepared to modify his or her approach accordingly.

The components we have described so far serve either to give direction or to provide an inducement and can only fulfil both functions if used in conjunction with each other. As we noted earlier, however, there are certain components which can fulfil both functions at the same time, if used skillfully. These are praise and criticism.

Praise Praise tells the subordinate that his or her performance is appreciated and admired by the manager. If the subordinate values praise from his or her manager, this is likely to increase the subordinate's self esteem, sense of achievement and feelings of doing something worthwhile and meaningful, which many people find highly motivating. Furthermore, if the praise is sufficiently detailed, it will let the subordinate know what kinds of things the manager thinks are praiseworthy and therefore are likely to be appreciated in future. For example:

> "I must congratulate you on the way you handled the fault on the stamping machine yesterday. If you hadn't been so alert and switched it off when you did, the whole machine might have seized up and we could have had a major repair job on our hands. As it was, we hardly lost any production at all. Well done!"

However, using praise effectively requires much more skill than is generally recognized. Praise, it has been said, should be *personal, proximate* and *precise*. In other words, an individual is more likely to respond to praise if it is directed towards him or her personally, if it is close in time to the event being praised, and if it describes in detail what the person has done which is worthy of being praised. It is the latter which seems to cause most difficulty. We all seem to be able to describe precisely and at length what someone has done wrong, but find it much less easy to tell someone in precise detail what he or she did right. Simply saying "Well done, keep up the good work" may let someone know that he or she is appreciated, but it does not tell the individual precisely what is appreciated. Furthermore, because general praise is so easy to give, there is a danger that it will be dismissed by the subordinate as 'mere flannel', whereas a manager would be unlikely to go to the trouble of praising in detail unless he or she actually meant it.

Similarly, praise without conviction is also likely to have little effect. Comments such as "Overall, your performance has been quite good over the past year", said in an off-hand manner is unlikely to have much influence on subordinates' level of motivation or subsequent behaviour. They are much more likely to be waiting for the inevitable ''but'' followed by the bad news. Simple rules, such as 'always precede blame with praise' are of little help if the subordinate knows that brief, weak and general praise is always followed by lengthy and detailed criticism. Again, the answer seems to be precision. If the manager identified precisely what the subordinate did which merits praise, and will not use it without specifying what this is, then the danger of weak general praise is considerably diminished.

Criticism Criticism lets the subordinate know that the manager is dissatisfied with his or her performance. Used effectively, it should also let the subordinate know what he or she should have done differently in order to avoid the criticism. For example:

"You should have shut down the stamping machine as soon as you realized a fault had developed. I realize that there was a chance that it might have lasted out until the end of the shift and saved us interrupting production. As things turned out, however, the whole machine seized up and we now have a major repair job on our hands. In future, remember that it is much better to close the machine down for repairs rather than risk a major breakdown.''

Like praise, criticism should be directed at a particular person as soon after the event as possible. Criticizing a whole group of people is likely to be ineffective, because at least some of them may feel, rightly or wrongly, that they were not at fault and are, therefore, being blamed unfairly. Similarly, criticizing someone long after the event serves little useful function. Whether criticism should be precise or not is another matter. If the person is already aware of what he or she did wrong and what should be done differently next time, then detailed criticism may simply cause resentment. This is not to say that the incident should be ignored. The subordinate may be waiting apprehensively for the manager's reaction, and feel very uneasy if nothing is said. However, a brief comment, such as "I know you must feel as badly about that as I do, but at least we know how to avoid the problem in future'' may be sufficient. On the other hand, if the person does not know precisely what he or she did which caused the problem or what to do differently to avoid it in future, then it may be necessary to provide more detailed feedback and guidance.

Like threats, criticism has the disadvantage of being likely to cause resentment and dissatisfaction. It can make the subordinate less cooperative in future, and less enthusiastic about the job generally. If alternative methods of solving the performance problem can be found, therefore, these should be seriously considered. Causal analysis is one possibility (see Chapter 6) as is non-evaluative feedback, i.e. pointing out the negative consequences of the subordinate's actions, without attaching specific blame. However, such methods may not always be appropriate. The subordinate may either not be able to identify what went wrong or may not accept personal responsibility for the consequences of his or her actions, blaming instead other people, bad luck, and so on. In this case, it is better for the manager to let the subordinate know that he or she is dissatisfied with the subordinate's actions, rather than to ignore the problem and risk the same thing happening again. However, two points should be made. Firstly, the criticism should only be in sufficient detail to ensure that the subordinate understands precisely what he or she did wrong. Secondly, the main emphasis should be on what can be done to avoid the problem arising again in future, and, where appropriate, what the manager can do to help the subordinate to achieve this improvement in performance. In other words, the criticism should be constructive.

Leading Questions The final technique for influencing behaviour superficially resembles an information gathering component. It is a form of question which signals quite clearly the answer which the respondent is expected to give. For example:

"You do realize how important it is to follow agreed safety procedures, don't you?"

"You do agree that absenteeism does give rise to serious problems in this department, don't you?"

"You would like to go on an interpersonal skills training course, wouldn't you?"

It would obviously be unwise to take affirmative answers to such quesions at face value. They could represent the subordinate's genuine opinions, but there is always the danger that the manager is simply being given the answer that he or she apparently wishes to hear. Thus leading questions are inappropriate as means of gathering information. Nevertheless, they can be of limited use as means of influencing behaviour. Agreement with a leading question cannot be taken to indicate the subordinate's wholehearted commitment to the idea being proposed by the manager, but they can be used simply as a means of obtaining explicit verbal agreement, either for the record or to provide the basis for a more detailed argument using other components such as requests, explanations, and orders.

A summary of the various components described in this section is given in Table 3.

HANDLING EMOTION

The third major purpose for which the skilful use of questions and statements may be required is the influencing of the subordinate's emotional reactions. Of particular importance is the ability to diminish or dispel adverse emotional reactions, such as anger, frustration, dissatisfaction, anxiety, despair, and so on. This may be required because subordinates themselves raise problems, with the manager, which are causing them to feel aggrieved or distressed. For example, the manager may be faced with an angry or resentful subordinate who believes that he or she has been badly treated, either by the manager or others within the organization. Another subordinate may feel anxious or depressed about domestic problems or difficulties at work and come to the manager for guidance

TABLE 3 Components for Influencing Behaviour
Components for Getting the Subordinate to Maintain a Satisfactory Level of Performance or to Do Something Differently to Improve It

Component	Appropriate use	Inappropriate use
Orders e.g. "Do it now" "... this is the way it will be done."	With staff who need or prefer clear, precise instructions. Where compliance is vital due to special circumstances e.g. time constraint, emergencies, etc.	Where the benefits do not justify any resentment or stifling of ideas which may result
Requests e.g. "I have a problem..." "Could you next time then, please..."	With subordinates who are more motivated by being asked or may contribute useful ideas to the problem	With subordinates who need or prefer clear, precise instructions
Advice/suggestions e.g. "You could improve on that by..." "The disadvantage of that is... ... but this way..."	With staff who prefer guidance and may be influenced in the desired direction by the 'logic of the situation', e.g. those lacking experience	Where compliance is essential and advice may be ignored
Promises e.g. "... then I'll give you the opportunity to tackle bigger projects."	Where the task may lack intrinsic reward and extrinsic reward must be introduced for motivational purposes	Where the promises cannot be fulfilled. When the subordinate will perform the task effectively anyway
Threats e.g. "... I will make you regret it" "... and I shall begin formal disciplinary proceedings."	Where compliance is essential and cannot otherwise be achieved, e.g. advice ignored, no available rewards, etc.	When more positive methods are available. Where threats cannot be fulfilled. When the subordinate would perform adequately anyway
Explanations e.g. "... because..." "The reason is that..."	With those subordinates who are more motivated by understanding the reasons for doing something	When the explanation will be rejected, leading to unproductive argument
Praise e.g. "I think that was well done because..."	To provide immediate feedback about the subordinate's standard of performance in a specific area and appreciation of it	If too general, imprecise or late. When used in a patronizing way without conviction
Criticism e.g. "Where you went wrong was... but this could be overcome by..."	To provide feedback on substandard performance in a particular area with emphasis on how to do it better next time	When used negatively without emphasis on how to do it better. When it is likely to impair performance further due to resentment aroused
Leading questions e.g. "You must agree that..." "Don't you think that..." "You **do** see the point why..."	To gain compliance or acceptance by signalling the expected answer. Can be used to emphasize or check on a point made	For encouraging a subordinate to express his/her views, feelings etc. With reticent staff. For gaining commitment

or reassurance. If the problem has a simple and immediate solution, it may be possible to alleviate the adverse emotional reaction by solving the problem itself. However, the problems which cause adults to experience strong emotional reactions often have no obvious or easy solution. It may be necessary to gather information to discover the exact nature of the problem and then explore the feasibility of several alternative solutions. Obviously, a subordinate who is highly emotionally aroused will not be capable of making a fully rational contribution to the solution of the problem. Thus, it is usually more effective to tackle the emotion first, and help the subordinate to reach a more calm and stable emotional state, before attempting to solve the problem itself.

Adverse emotional reactions may also occur as a reaction to the manager's attempt to influence subordinates' work performance. For example, a subordinate may resent the implication that some aspect of his or her work performance is not up to standard, or feel that he or she is being criticized too harshly for a minor failing or for something which was not his or her fault. Such reactions will make it much more difficult to bring about the desired performance improvement. Subordinates who are angry and aggrieved are much less likely to listen to what the manager has to say, less capable of analyzing the situation logically, and more likely to raise objections and present counterarguments. In a limited number of cases, it may be appropriate to override such objections and insist that the manager's viewpoint is accepted. An example might be a disciplinary interview where the facts are clear and the problem has been thoroughly discussed on previous occasions. In most cases, however, it will be much more effective to resolve the emotional problem first, and dissipate the subordinate's anger or resentment before proceeding with further attempts to tackle the performance problem. Unless this is done, it is likely to take the manager much longer to gain acceptance of his or her views, at best reluctant compliance will be obtained, and there may still be unresolved feelings of bitterness which could adversely affect future relations with the manager.

What steps, then, can be taken to resolve such emotional problems? First of all, the manager should avoid using insensitive words or phrases which might aggravate the emotional reactions. Comments about the subordinate's "lack of judgement", "carelessness", "abrasive manner", "mistakes", "failure", "faults", "weaknesses", and so on, can only make things worse, and may even trigger an adverse emotional reaction in the first place. It appears that skilled negotiators even avoid using positive descriptions of themselves which could irritate the other party by implying that they do not possess these character- istics. For example, describing oneself as fair and reasonable has the implication that the other party is *un*fair and *un*reasonable.[5]

Secondly, there are certain behavioural influence components which can be used to diminish adverse emotional reactions. One can *promise* to do something to resolve the underlying problem. As we have already noted, however, this should only be done if the subordinate has a reasonable and equitable case. If this is not so, then the subordinate is being rewarded for being difficult, and other less difficult subordinates are likely to feel resentful because they are not being similarly rewarded. Similarly, where the negative reaction has occurred because the subordinate has not fully understood the circumstances involved, then an *explanation* of the true situation may serve to resolve the problem. On the other hand, if the subordinate is highly aggrieved, then attempting to 'explain away' the problem may have the opposite effect to that intended. The apparently reasonable explanation may simply give the subordinate additional opportunities to express anger and resentment. To accept the explanation would mean that there was no need to get so upset in the first place, which is in itself annoying and thus is likely to lead to complaints that the subordinate should have been kept informed at the very least.

Other techniques for dealing with high emotion may therefore be required. The two main ones are apologies and reflectives.

Apologies If the manager is in some way responsible for the subordinate's adverse emotional reaction, then a firm and sincere apology can help to alleviate the situation, particularly if combined with a constructive discussion of ways of avoiding similar problems arising in future. For example:

"I really am sorry about that. I must make sure it doesn't happen again. How do you think we can . . ."

If the subordinate is extremely aroused, however, even an apology may not be sufficient to dispel or dissipate the negative feelings. Like an explanation, it may simply provide the subordinate with additional targets against which to express anger or dissatisfaction.

Reflectives The reflective is a complex and sophisticated technique, but is probably more useful than any other as a means of handling high emotion. The manager who is confronted with a subordinate in a highly emotional and antagonistic state is faced with a dilemma. What can he or she do which will effectively lower the level of emotional arousal? Disagreeing with the person in any way will almost certainly cause even greater anger, or at the very least invite further expression of the subordinate's grievances. If the manager simply uses his or her authority and tells the subordinate to shut up, this may work, but it could equally lead to an even greater confrontation, and in any case is likely to sour the relationship. Agreeing with the subordinate may reduce the level of emotional arousal, but obviously this is not an appropriate step if the manager does not fully accept the subordinate's viewpoint, and would lead to a commitment which the manager could regret. What is needed, therefore, is a neutral statement, which provides no further incentive to anger, and which will allow the emotion to burn itself out. The reflective achieves this by reflecting back the emotional content of what the other person is saying, in a concerned and non-evaluative way. For example:

Subordinate: "That's typical. I try to do my job effectively and all you can do is criticize me for some minor infringement of company regulations. That's the final straw. From now on you can worry about maintenance problems. If the machine breaks down and we have to wait two months for spares, that's your problem, not mine. I don't see why I should worry. No one else does!"

Manager: "You seem to be very upset about this."

Subordinate: "Of course I'm upset. I do my best for the company. I get no thanks when things go right, but as soon as I ignore one petty rule, I get criticized out of all proportion."

Manager: "You feel that you don't get enough recognition for the work you do."

Subordinate: "No I don't. You look at the other people. They do the bare minimum. If a machine breaks down, they just call in Maintenance. They don't care how long it takes to put right. I try to run things efficiently. I try to be prepared for emergencies, and what happens? Instead of thanking me for all the extra work I put in, all you can do is criticize."

Manager: "And you find that demoralizing because it seems unfair."

Subordinate: "Yes, it does. I think the company should give more recognition to the people who have the company's interests at heart. I'm not saying I'm the only one—there are others—but . . ."

Presented as they are here, without any indication of the way in which they are said, such reflectives may appear artificial or trivial. It may also appear that they would stimulate the subordinate to become more angry by encouraging him or her to comment further on the situation. However, the reverse is the case. By simply reflecting back the subordinate's emotion, the manager is encouraging the subordinate to explain and justify his or her anger. In doing this, the subordinate is using reason. Because the manager is not introducing further irritants to arouse the anger once again, reason gradually takes over as the anger dissipates. Once the subordinate has returned to a more stable emotional state, the manager can then move to other techniques in an attempt to find a solution to the problem. Until the emotion has been dissipated, however, there is little point in trying to find a rational solution to the problem because the subordinate is unlikely to be willing or able to discuss things rationally. The skilful use of reflectives can provide a particularly effective way of defusing such highly charged emotional situations and channelling the discussion towards a more rational examination of the problem.

Reflectives can also be useful as a means of bringing out into the open feelings which are being expressed at a low level, but still appear to have an adverse effect on the interaction. For example:

"You don't seem very enthusiastic about the idea."
"I seem to sense a certain reluctance on your part."
"I get the impression that you are rather annoyed about something."

By bringing such negative feelings out into the open the manager may be able to solve the problem and eliminate some source of doubt, fear or irritation which would otherwise prevent a fully constructive discussion from taking place. Reflectives can also be used to encourage someone to talk about more positive emotions. For example:

"You must be very pleased about that."
"So everything worked out just as you had planned it, then?"

Just as people find it difficult to be rational about something when they are angry, they may also find it difficult to concentrate on other things whilst experiencing a positive emotion. Thus, if the manager wishes to have a serious discussion on some topic, it would be better to allow time for the positive emotion to burn itself out, and perhaps encourage it to do so using reflectives, rather than to try to impose on the subordinate an abrupt change of mood. Using reflectives may seem time consuming, but they are likely to achieve the desired effect much more quickly than trying to stop the emotion by other means.

It must be pointed out, however, that the appropriate use of reflectives is probably the most difficult of all the techniques we have described in this chapter. It requires high level listening and diagnostic skill to identify the person's exact feelings and the reasons for them. It requires the ability to feed these back to the person in a concerned way, without revealing one's own evaluation of the situation or the person. It also requires the ability to take personal criticism, or perhaps even abuse, without reacting to it defensively or emotionally.

Components for handling emotion are summarized in Table 4.

So far, we have mainly been concerned with defusing negative emotional reactions. However, there are also times when a manager may wish to raise the level of emotion amongst subordinates. The manager may not only wish subordinates to be less angry, resentful or frustrated, but may want them to be more enthusiastic, aggressive, happy, proud, confident, or perhaps even fearful. It is less easy to identify specific verbal components which are concerned with raising peoples' level of emotional arousal. We suspect that such techniques typically involve using the behavioural influence components which have already described in a particular way, rather than a separate set of components. Thus blood curdling threats, generous promises, fulsome praise are obviously intended to produce a greater emotional response than would occur if the same

TABLE 4 Components for Handling Emotion
Components for Defusing the Situation to Enable the Interaction to Proceed on a More Rational Basis

Component	Appropriate use	Inappropriate use
Apologies e.g. "First of all I must apologize for . . ." "I'm **very** sorry, I didn't realize . . ."	When used confidently and constructively to eliminate a source of grievance which might inhibit rational discussion	If too abject, off-hand or patronizing
Reflectives e.g. "You seem upset about . . ." "You feel it would be unfair to . . ." (i.e. reflecting back the **emotional** content of what is expressed)	To indicate, without evaluation, a concerned awareness of the subordinate's emotions or frustrations and to provide an opportunity to discharge these by letting the subordinate work through the problem(s)	If used evaluatively, reproachfully or disparagingly. Where manager cannot handle criticism or abuse. In situations of severe time constraint. For checking particular points of information or fact

things were said in a more matter of fact way. In the next chapter, we will examine the significant role played by such nonverbal cues in manager–subordinate interactions.

At the end of this chapter there are three sets of exercises. The first two are intended to allow managers to assess their ability to recognize different types of questions and statements and the situations in which their use is most appropriate. The third provides the opportunity to practise formulating appropriate reflectives. Answers are given in Appendices II and III.

REFERENCES

1   GA Randall, PMA Packard, RL Shaw and AJ Slater (1972), *Staff Appraisal*, Institute of Personnel Management.

2   JP Zima (1971), 'Counselling Concepts for Supervisors', *Personnel Journal*, Vol. 50, pp. 482–485.

3   CI Hovland, IL Janis and HH Kelley (1953), *Communication and Persuasion*, Yale University Press, pp. 270–271.

4   H Levinthal, R Singer and S Jones (1965), 'Effects of Fear and Specificity of Recommendation Upon Attitudes and Behaviour', *Journal of Personality and Social Psychology*, Vol. 2, pp. 20–29.

5   N Rackham and J Carlysle (1978) 'The Effective Negotiator. Part 1: The Behaviour of Successful Negotiators', *Journal of European Industrial Training*, Vol. 2, pp. 6–11.

RECOGNIZING QUESTION AND STATEMENT TYPES

(Answers are given in Appendix II.)
Below are listed several questions and statements. Classify each one as belonging to one of the following types.

Closed	Comparison	Hypothetical	Leading	Multiple
Bridges	Lubricators	Open	Probing	Reflective	Summary

Question/Statement

A Tell me how you intend to go about reducing the number of accidents in the department? . . . .

B You do keep the safety manual in an accessible place don't you? . . . .

C You feel frustrated because you can't get people to realize the importance of following safety regulations. . . . .

D How many accidents were there in your department last year? That is, how many accidents were there which resulted in time off work and what was the average length of time they stayed off work? . . . .

E What seems to have emerged from the discussion so far is that the safety training is successful with the younger employees, but the older ones seem to be giving less priority to putting it into practice. . . . .

F Do you think that safety training is more effectively carried out in the workplace or in the training department? . . . .

G How many working days were lost through accidents in your department last month? . . . .

H What precisely has he done which makes you say he isn't sufficiently safety conscious? . . . .

I What would you do if you saw one of your subordinates breaking safety regulations? . . . .

J I see . . . yes . . . go on . . . mmm. . . . .

K We have agreed that you will check with Personnel about the availability of safety posters, now can we move on to discuss safety training. . . . .

APPROPRIATE USE OF QUESTION AND STATEMENT TYPES

(Answers are given in Appendix II.)
Which of the questions and statements from the previous Exercise would be most appropriate in the following circumstances?
For example, if you think that question C would be most appropriate for the purpose of no. 1 below, then write C on the right-hand side of the page. If you think two or more are appropriate then write all the appropriate letters.

For the Purpose of: **Most Appropriate**

1 Introducing a topic, encouraging the subordinate to talk and gathering information on a broad basis.

2 Getting the subordinate to explore and reveal his own needs, values, etc.

3 Gaining the subordinate's acceptance of your view, usually in the form of compliance rather than commitment.

4 Getting the subordinate to think about previously unconsidered areas.

5 Dealing with emotionally charged statements.

6 Providing a smooth link between one topic and another.

7 Encouraging the subordinate to continue talking and expand his views without interrupting his flow of words.

8 Establishing specific facts which only require short answers.

9 Ensuring that details are not forgotten, and gaining commitment to a plan of action.

10 Encouraging the subordinate to give more precise and detailed information.

DEALING WITH EMOTION AND FRUSTRATION

In dealing with expressions of frustration and emotion, there is a tendency to attempt to solve the problem for the emotional or frustrated individual. Although commendable, the intention is rarely successful. Attempts to solve the problem by using such things as premature advice ("What you need to do is . . .") or self disclosure ("I had similar problems when I first came here, but what I did was . . .") usually fail to do what is probably most required, to let the individual 'get it off his or her chest'. To do this requires the manager to try to see and understand the problem from the subordinate's own frame of reference. This usually results in the aggrieved person releasing his or her emotion or frustration and will eventually lead to a more rational, problem solving situation. The manager will be seen to be demonstrating an attempt at understanding by attending to, listening and verbally responding in such a way that shows interest and concern in the subordinate's problems.

Below are a number of statements, intended to express emotion or frustration, followed by a number of possible responses. Read the responses and decide which one is trying to indicate interest and concern and which one is a poor response. Try to give reasons for your decision (e.g. shows disrespect, premature advice, irrelevant self disclosure, or shows concern and is likely to encourage the subordinate to comment further).

Example

"Sandra Smith has it in for me. Even since I started this job she's been at me. I behave just like the other operators but when something goes wrong she always checks what I was doing first".

(a) "Just try and ignore it. Don't go and do anything stupid or you might be in worse trouble."

Poor response because it gives premature advice and attempts to stop any further expression of emotion and frustration.

(b) "You feel she's being unfair to you and don't like it."
Good response because it reflects back the problem and is likely to elicit further comment.
(c) "You say she's always at you. Have you done something to upset her?"
Poor response because it is expressing disbelief in what has been said—it is judgemental.
(d) "We all get problems like this at times and it makes life that bit more difficult. If you stay cool, she'll stop eventually. Now, have you finished that special assignment?"
Poor response because it is placating, shows inappropriate sympathy, gives premature advice and attempts to change the subject.

Now try these for yourself. (Answers are given in Appendix III.)

1   "I feel just like a slave around here. I was employed as a shorthand-typist and yet I'm expected to make tea and coffee, do the shopping and stay around during lunchtime and hometime in case something needs doing at short notice. Last night I didn't get home 'till nearly 7 o'clock."
    (a)   "I'm sorry about last night. Did you have something special on?"
    (b)   "I understand how you feel but often it's not anyones fault, especially if there's an urgent order to be completed."
    (c)   "I'm sorry, but the person before you really liked getting involved and I assumed you would too."
    (d)   "You resent being expected to do things which you don't think are part of your job."

2   "I don't know if it's me or not. Over the last two years we've hired a lot of young people. They're all polite to me, but that's about it. I can't seem to find out what makes them tick. I don't understand them and I find it hard to establish any kind of relationship with them."
    (a)   "You don't seem to know where the fault lies".
    (b)   "You're having difficulty handling your subordinates".
    (c)   "You feel somewhat isolated from them and it's puzzling you".
    (d)   "What do you think I can do to help?"

3   "If it keeps on like this we'll go under. The shop stewards in my department are giving me hell. If I try to move people around there's an uproar. With the company the way it is and pressure on me to improve productivity, I've just got to have more leeway to run the department more efficiently."
    (a)   "You're feeling under pressure from both management and shop stewards and it's affecting your efforts to organize the work."
    (b)   "Could you elaborate on that a little more."
    (c)   "You've got to use more discipline. Take away their privileges if they don't do as you want them."
    (d)   "OK it's hard on you but if we keep our heads we can work something out. Let's see if we can sort it out."

For the last two examples, construct your own response.

4   "I really find it hard to work for him. He's so inconsistent. I seem to be getting along fine then for no apparent reason he blows up. I just don't know where I am with him."

5   "Do you know, I've really enjoyed working here for the past three months. The work's really interested me and I get a lot of satisfaction out of doing it."

Chapter 5

Nonverbal Components of Manager–Subordinate Interactions

INTRODUCTION

Face-to-face communication is very much a multichannel process. We not only hear the words said, but also register the other person's tone of voice, facial expression, body posture, gestures, proximity, and so on. These nonverbal cues may act to supplement, modify, contradict, or even at time replace the actual words spoken.

To illustrate this point, let's consider some examples.

> "That's interesting."
> "Would you go and see Jones in Duplicating and make sure that the copies of my report will be ready for this afternoon's meeting."
> "I'm sorry about that; I must make sure it doesn't happen again."

The impact of the first statement is likely to be enhanced if it is said in a lively tone of voice, with an animated expression, whilst leaning forward and looking the other person in the eye. On the other hand, the same statement said in a flat tone of voice, with a neutral expression, whilst leaning back and staring out of the window, presents a contradictory message. Whilst the words express interest, the nonverbal cues say the opposite. Research evidence suggests that, of the two, the nonverbal cues are more likely to be believed. It has been estimated that feelings are communicated 55% by facial expression, 38% by tone of voice and only 7% by the actual words used.[1] Furthermore, there is evidence that the less obvious nonverbal cues, such as body posture, provide a more accurate indication of an individual's true feelings, because these are the ones which people take least trouble to disguise when not being truthful.[2]

Nonverbal cues may also be indicative of several other factors in an interaction, such as the friendliness and the relative status or power of the people concerned. The request to go and see Jones in Duplicating could be said in a harsh, domineering tone of voice, with aggressive facial expression and body posture, making it the equivalent of an order, and an unpleasant one at that, or it could be said in a pleading tone, with abject facial expression and body posture, turning it into a humble request.

Similarly, the apology in the third example, could be said in at least three different ways:

- in a low tone, with eyes cast down, an unhappy facial expression, hunched shoulders, and fidgeting hands
- in a clear firm tone of voice, with direct eye contact, an interested facial expression, squared shoulders, leaning slightly forward, and slightly clenched hands
- in a slightly irritable tone of voice, looking over the person's shoulder, with a disinterested facial expression, relaxed body posture, leaning slightly backward, and with a negligent wave of the hand.

The first is likely to be seen as an abject apology by someone of lower status pleading not to be punished. The second is more likely to be seen as a sincere expression of regret and a credible commitment to rectify the situation. The third is more likely to be seen as someone of superior status or power, attempting to get rid of a 'trivial' problem by making an insincere expression of regret and a promise which probably will not be kept.

These examples illustrate two of the main problems which may arise in handling nonverbal cues. Firstly, managers may not realize that they are sending contradictory nonverbal messages alongside their intended verbal ones and reducing or even negating their impact. Secondly, they may not realize that by varying their nonverbal cues, they can sometimes change the tone of what they are saying to beneficial effect. For example, they may be able to change an order into a request, which is more acceptable to a subordinate, but no less compelling, or apologize to a subordinate without appearing to demean themselves or running the risk of loss of authority.

A third problem, not illustrated, is that of failing to observe nonverbal cues from the subordinate, and we will return to this later.

It is apparent that nonverbal communication takes many different forms. Virtually anything a human being does could, under some circumstances, communicate something to an observer. Thus, potentially, nonverbal communication could cover all human behaviour except for the spoken and written word. Not surprisingly therefore, researchers in the area have found it difficult to develop an agreed classification system which encompasses all types of nonverbal communication. Based on this research,[3] however, we have produced our own list by concentrating upon those aspects which are of greatest relevance to manager–subordinate interactions. For convenience, we have grouped these under three headings—facial, vocal and physical (see Table 5).

Given that all these different aspects of behaviour are potential sources of information about an individual, the next question we need to answer is precisely what do they communicate. Traditionally, nonverbal communication has been primarily regarded as a way of showing or revealing emotions. More recent research shows that it also serves several other functions. For example, it helps to regulate interactions between people, by letting the participants know when someone wishes to speak, hand over the speaker's role to someone else, continue listening, and so on. It can indicate the relative status or power of the

TABLE 5 Nonverbal Components in Manager–Subordinate Interactions

Facial	**For Example**
Facial expression	smiles, raised eyebrows, wrinkled forehead, wide open eyes, lightly closed mouth
Direction of gaze	direct eye contact, downcast eyes
Vocal	
Acoustic	pitch and loudness
Voice qualities	nasal, raspy
Pauses and hesitations	gaps in verbal messages
Speech tempo and rhythm	drawling, staccato
Vocalizations	"um", "er", "ah"
Physical	
Head movements	nodding, shaking
Gestures	movement of the hands and arms, such as clenching the fist, making chopping motions with the hand, waving, shrugging shoulders
Postures	hands on hips, arms or legs crossed, leaning forward or backward, hunched shoulders
Posture shifts	changing one's position in a chair, crossing and uncrossing one's arms or legs
Continuous movements	swinging one's foot, scratching one's arm, playing with a pencil
Distance between people	too close, comfortable, too far
Body orientation	face to face with another person, at right angles

people who are interacting. It can reflect the complexity of the verbal message the person is attempting to communicate, and his or her difficulty in expressing it. Finally, in a limited number of cases, nonverbal signals can act as a substitute for explicitly verbal messages, e.g. a nod can stand for "yes", and a shrug of the shoulders for "I don't know".

As we pointed out earlier, virtually any aspect of an individual's nonverbal behaviour can, in some circumstances, act as a source of nonverbal communication, whether intentional or unintentional. The problem from our point of view, however, is that different aspects of nonverbal behaviour differ considerably in their *reliability* as a source of information from or about the person concerned. That is, some forms of nonverbal behaviour represent the same thing relatively consistently, whilst others may represent different things in different situations or when performed by different individuals. For example, certain facial expressions represent particular emotions with a high degree of consistency, even across different cultures.[4] On the other hand, activities such as scratching the back of one's hand or swinging one's foot may be a sign of nervousness in one person, whilst another may perform them habitually irrespective of emotional state. In fact, according to Dittman,[5] "there are a few body movements that behave like coded material in that they are easily understood by all or most members of the community. By far the greater majority of movements, however, serve more as cues from which we make inferences. If all the cues add up right, our guesses from these messages can be very good ones, but usually we don't have time for much inferring if we are to keep up with the conversation. With few exceptions", Dittman concludes, "we cannot look at a person's movements and know definitely what they mean in body language".

Let us examine some of the forms of nonverbal behaviour which do reliably communicate something which could be of significance in manager–subordinate interactions.

FUNCTIONS OF NONVERBAL COMMUNICATION

Substitutes for Verbal Messages

As noted previously, even in people without hearing or speaking difficulties, there are a few nonverbal signals which can act as substitutes for explicit verbal messages. Examples include a nod for "yes", a shake of the head for "no" and shrugging the shoulders for "I don't know". They can, of course, also accompany such verbal messages, but they are comprehensible on their own. Even these relatively explicit signs can have different meanings according to context. For example, nodding ones head whilst someone else is talking can be the equivalent of "Mm-hm", "I see", and so on. Similarly, the head shake performed continuously whilst saying something complimentary (e.g. "There was really beautiful photography in that movie") can indicate a positive attitude rather than a negative one.[6] Nevertheless, these do not constitute serious sources of ambiguity, as the meaning can be deduced from the context, just as we can deduce the meaning of similar sounding words, such as 'bough' and 'bow', from their verbal context.

Emotions

According to Ekman,[7] experiments over the past fifty years have produced "consistent and conclusive evidence that accurate judgements of facial expression can be made". In particular, six emotions—happiness, sadness, surprise, fear, anger and disgust—can be recognized with a high degree of reliability. Furthermore, the facial expressions associated with these emotions seem to be the same even for people from different cultures. Eckman comments that there are probably other emotions conveyed by the face, such as shame, interest and excitement, but these have not yet been as firmly established by research.

Where people do differ, however, is in the extent to which they display such emotions or in the circumstances in which they will display them. Some people may show their emotions readily, whilst others may block the facial expression of particular emotions such as anger, or in extreme cases may be poker-faced never revealing in their faces how they feel. Similarly, some people may block the expression of an emotion in one situation, such as never allowing themselves to show anger in front of customers or superiors, but allow themselves to show the same emotion in other situations. Furthermore, it is of course possible to fake emotions which we do not feel ("Thank you for a *lovely* dinner party Mrs Jones, it was *most* enjoyable!") and people vary in the extent to which they can do this convincingly. Whilst it is possible to judge genuine facial expressions accurately therefore, two reservations need to be noted. The fact that someone is not displaying emotion is not necessarily a sign that they are not experiencing it, and the fact the someone is displaying an emotion need not necessarily indicate that they are *genuinely* experiencing it.

Facial expressions provide us with our main source of information concerning emotion. As we have already noted, emotion is judged much more by facial expression than by tone of voice. Nevertheless, tone of voice does provide us with some useful information concerning emotions.[8] Furthermore it appears that some emotions are more easily recognized by means of vocal cues than others. For example, it has been found that whilst visual cues are particularly helpful in making judgements about happiness, vocal cues are particularly useful in making judgements about anxiety.[9] There is evidence that anxiety is associated with such vocal cues as superfluous repetition of words or phrases, incomplete sentences, rephrasing of sentences, omission of words or parts of words, and "ahs", "ers" and "mms", etc.[10]

Liking, Friendliness and Warmth

Apart from the primary emotions so far discussed, a variety of nonverbal cues also indicate liking, friendliness or warmth towards another person. These include nodding, smiling, greater eye contact, leaning forward, standing or sitting closer, and standing or sitting at a slight angle to the other person.[11] It is, of course, possible to overdo any of these cues, e.g. by standing too close to the person concerned or staring fixedly, in which case they may become unpleasant or embarrassing. If it is impossible to retreat physically from the situation, the other person is then likely to take measures to reduce the level of intimacy, such as decreased eye contact, turning away, leaning back, blocking the presence of the other person with the hand or elbow, and so on. Self manipulative behaviours, such as scratching or rubbing the hand are also likely to increase.[12] Finally, it is worth noting that many of the cues which indicate liking may also indicate attention to the other person or interest in what they are saying. Examples include nodding and greater eye contact, but there are also vocal cues such as saying "mm-mm", etc.

Status, Power and Dominance

There are numerous nonverbal signals which indicate which of two or more people has the higher status, more power or is more dominant. An important one is the amount of time people spend looking at each other during conversation. It has been found that subordinates look at superiors more whilst the superior is talking than superiors look at subordinate whilst the subordinate is talking. Furthermore, subordinates look at superiors more whilst listening to them than when talking to them, and superiors tend to look at subordinates more when talking to them than whilst listening to them.[13] These patterns of behaviour also influence other people's assessment of the power of the person concerned, so that people who look more whilst speaking and less whilst listening are seen as being more powerful, and vice versa.[14] Other research suggests lower status people respond more quickly when talking to higher status people, but there are more pauses whilst they are talking,[15] perhaps because they are searching for the 'right' thing to say.

As noted earlier, vocal cues are particularly important in relation to certain types of emotion. Another area where they are important is in the communication of dominance and assertiveness. It has been found that whilst visual cues are used more in judging how pleasant or agreeable someone is, vocal cues are used more, and are more useful, in judging dominance and assertiveness. This seems to be because there is a single visual cue, the smile, which reliably indicates how positive the person feels, but no visual cues which so reliably indicate dominance. Conversely, it seems that the vocal cue of loudness may be an effective cue for conveying dominance, but not how pleasant people are.[16]

Finally, seating arrangements may indicate something about the relationship between the people involved in an interaction. People were asked how they would sit at a table with another person in different social situations. In competitive situations, the vast majority of people chose to sit opposite each other, whereas in cooperative situations, more people chose to sit on the same side of the table. Where the situation was described as simply involving a conversation, the most popular seating arrangement was diagonally across the corner of the table.[17]

Regulation of Verbal Communication

An important class of nonverbal cues, known as 'regulators', serve the function of regulating and integrating the exchange of verbal information in an interaction. These regulators, according to Ekman and Friesen,[18] "tell the speaker to continue, repeat, elaborate, hurry up, become more interesting, less salacious, give the other a chance to talk, etc. They can tell the listener to pay special attention, to wait just a minute to talk, etc." Again, it is impossible to specify all the nonverbal cues which might indicate such things. Rosenfeld[19] gives examples of nonverbal cues which might fulfil each of the above functions—silent attention or small periodic nods, a cocking of the head while cupping the ear, a puzzled expression, rapid head nods, yawning, opening the mouth and raising a hand, tapping the listener with a finger, raising the hand (to signal 'wait'). As virtually any category of nonverbal behaviour can act as a regulator in some circumstances, however, this list could be extended almost indefinitely.

Nevertheless, it is possible to identify some of the major cues which contribute to the smooth transition between speaker and listener roles. Such switches commonly take place at junctures which mark the end of a segment of speech, particularly if followed by a pause. It is here that most nonverbal cues occur, signalling that the speaker wishes to stop talking or say more, or that the listener wishes the speaker to continue talking or give the listener the opportunity to say something.[20]

Cues that the speaker wishes the other person to take over the speaking role include turning the towards the listener, a rising or falling pitch at the end of a segment of speech, drawl on the final or stressed syllable, pausing, the termination of any hand gesture or the relaxation of a tense hand position, and phrases such as "and so on" or "you know". Conversely, cues that the speaker wishes to continue talking include looking away from the listener during a pause in speech, filling pauses with "ahs", "ums", etc. and a hand gesture which is not returned to rest during a pause.

Cues that the listener wishes to say something include turning the head away from the speaker, the start of a hand gesture, overloudness and a sharp, audible inhalation. Conversely, the listener may indicate that he or she wishes the speaker to continue talking by nodding and saying such things as "mm-hmm", "uh-huh", "I see" or "that's true". Such cues, along with smiling may also indicate understanding of, or agreement with, what the speaker is saying, and the speaker may occasionally solicit such cues from the listener by turning the head towards the listener, a rise or fall of pitch, and pausing. The lack of responses from the listener indicating understanding or agreement is likely to be unsettling to the speaker, who may either 'dry up' or repeat, elaborate or modify previous comments in an attempt to make them more acceptable or more comprehensible.[21]

The nonverbal cues we have been discussing do not, of course, invariably produce an orderly flow of information in conversations. People may not notice each others' nonverbal cues or may interpret them incorrectly. As such cues are often both low level and ambiguous, they are particularly subject to the kinds of perceptual distortion discussed in the Chapter 3. Alternatively, the speaker and listener may disagree about when they should change roles, and thus deliberately ignore clear signals from the other person. According to the type of cue being disregarded, this will lead either to unwanted and perhaps embarrassing silences or to interruptions and simultaneous speech.

Difficulty of Expressing Verbal Messages

Finally, it is worth noting that certain cues are indicative of the fact that the speaker is having difficulty expressing what he or she wishes to say. These include decreased eye contact, hesitation, silent pauses, speech disruptions, and so on.[22]

IMPLICATIONS FOR MANAGER—SUBORDINATE INTERACTIONS

The implications of nonverbal communication for manager—subordinate interactions can be examined under two main headings. Firstly, there are the nonverbal signals which the manager deliberately or inadvertently sends to subordinates, and their likely responses. Secondly, there is the extent to which the manager notices and correctly interprets the nonverbal cues exhibited by subordinates.

Nonverbal Cues Exhibited by the Manager

From the point of view of the manager's own nonverbal behaviour, the main implications are as follows:

- It is important to display nonverbal cues which are consistent with the verbal messages being sent. Inconsistency between verbal and nonverbal messages is likely to be interpreted as a sign of insincerity or deception, and it is the nonverbal message which is the more likely to be believed. It may well be that the manager experiences the emotions or attitudes being expressed verbally, e.g. enthusiasm, warmth, attention, but is simply not *displaying* them. As Hall[23] puts it, being a nice person is not a skill. But success at showing you are a nice person and doing so convincingly does reflect a skill! The same might be said for showing that one is a determined, aggressive person who will stand no nonsense, and doing so convincingly.

- In the case of the facial expressions which express emotion, these appear to be innate, and it is therefore simply a matter of displaying the appropriate emotion.

- An appearance of friendliness, warmth and attention can be increased by such cues as smiling, greater eye contact, standing or sitting closer, etc., or decreased by smiling less, giving less eye contact, etc. Because of individual and cultural differences, it is impossible to give ideal frequencies or distances with respect to such cues. For example, there is evidence that extroverts, in contrast with introverts, tend not only to sit closer to others, but to adopt positions which allow greater eye contact. Similarly, Arabs, Latin American and Mediterranean people tend in general to prefer closer speaking distances than British, North European and North American people.[24]

  As we noted earlier, however, overdoing signs of friendliness, warmth and attention to the extent that they become uncomfortable to the other person is likely to produce characteristic 'retreat' behaviours, such as avoiding eye contact, leaning back, etc. Providing managers are aware of such responses therefore, they can modify their own behaviour accordingly so that an acceptable balance is attained.

- The outward signs of differences in status and power can be manipulated in a number of ways. Managers can indicate that they wish to minimize the effect of status and power differences in the interaction by talking more softly, looking more at the subordinates whilst the latter are talking, glancing away more whilst they are themselves talking, and arranging seating positions so that chairs are on the same side of the table or diagonally across the corner of the table. Such nonverbal cues would be appropriate in situations where the manager wishes to show concern, gather information in a considerate way or solve problems participatively (see 'Ask–Listen' and 'Problem Solving' approaches to manager–subordinate interactions in Chapter 7). Conversely, the manager may wish to emphasize differences in rank e.g. in a disciplinary interview. In this case, speaking louder, increased eye contact whilst the manager is talking, decreased eye contact whilst the subordinate is talking and a seating arrangement with chairs on the opposite side of the table would be more appropriate (see 'Tell' and 'Tell–Sell' approaches in Chapter 7).

- Finally, there exist a variety of cues which managers can use to indicate that they wish subordinates to continue talking or allow the manager to speak. In our experience it is the former which is more likely to cause problems for the manager. On our courses, we rarely find that managers have difficulty in giving quite clear signals that they wish to take over the speaking role. Failing all else, if the subordinate ignores such cues, the manager can say loudly and explicitly "No, you can have your turn later. For the moment I am going to have my say". The more common problem is the manager who wishes to keep a subordinate talking but does not use the appropriate nonverbal cues, with the result that the subordinate eventually dries up or gives shorter and shorter responses. This situation can be rectified by asking the appropriate questions, e.g. open questions, comparisons, etc., and then following this by the relevant nonverbal cues such as nodding, smiling, leaning forward, eye contact and so on. Also important is the ability to tolerate silence. A pause is sometimes a sign that the other person wishes to relinquish the speakers role. On the other hand, pauses may also be a sign that the person is having difficulty phrasing what he or she wishes to say and they also occur more frequently when people of lower status are talking to higher status people. It seems likely, therefore, that the combination of these two factors will provide managers with greater opportunities to take over the speaker's role, which may at times lead to useful information being lost.

Interpretation of Nonverbal Cues Exhibited by the Subordinate

Turning to the manager's observation and interpretation of the subordinate's nonverbal behaviour, here it is much more difficult to draw clear cut conclusions due to individual and cultural differences and the inherent ambiguity of some nonverbal cues. Nevertheless, there are some nonverbal cues which are relatively unambiguous, e.g. the facial expression of genuine emotions. Thus the problem here is one of attention. Such cues can be interpreted correctly provided the manager watches out for them, but they can be missed if not attended to. In other cases, nonverbal cues may be ambiguous, either because they could indicate different things or because they are contradictory (e.g. verbal and facial expression of interest combined with a disinterested tone of voice). Thus such cues merely indicate that something *might* be happening rather than that something specific and identifiable *is* happening. Under such circumstances, however, it is possible to check verbally to establish precisely what the nonverbal cues mean, if indeed they mean anything at all. Reflectives are particularly useful for this purpose. For example, one might say "You look a little pained. Has something I've said upset you". The answer might be, given the ambiguity of many nonverbal cues, "Oh no, It's just that I have suddenly got cramp in my foot." If so, nothing is lost. On the other hand, such a question might bring out into the open, and defuse, a feeling of resentment which might otherwise have had an adverse effect on the remainder of the interaction.

Again, however, the question of attention is important. As we have already noted, low level cues are particularly susceptible to being distorted in the direction of the perceiver's needs and expectations. A typical example from one of the author's training groups went as follows:

Manager: "You would like to go on a human relations course, wouldn't you?" (A leading question, said with enthusiasm)

Subordinate: "Well, er, yes . . . if you say so." (Said hesitantly, in a low voice, with a slight shrug of the shoulders)

Manager: "Good I'm glad you agree. I'll fix that up. Now, another thing I wanted to talk to you about . . ."

When asked afterwards whether he thought the subordinate was enthusiastic about the human relations course, the manager said that he thought he was. He was then asked to listen to a tape recording of the above passage and asked whether he still thought the subordinate was enthusiastic. The manager said: "No, he isn't is he? It's obvious when you listen to it, isn't it? I can't understand how I missed it at the time". Part of the answer undoubtedly was lack of attention. The manager was busily thinking about the next topic he wished to raise and only half listening to the subordinate. In addition, however, the manager expected the subordinate to agree, and also wanted him to agree, because that would solve one of his problems. Thus the scene was ideally set, by the manager himself, to miss important nonverbal cues which were more revealing of the subordinate's true feelings than the actual words spoken.

Also important are the cues of wishing to take over, maintain or relinquish the speakers role. Not noticing or deliberately ignoring such cues can result in the manager continually interrupting the subordinate before the latter has finished what he or she wishes to say. This can, as already noted, result in important information being lost, and also lead to considerable resentment from subordinates who feel that they have not been given a fair opportunity to state their case.

It is worth noting that we are not suggesting that managers should be good at reading nonverbal cues simply because this will enable them to be more considerate in their behaviour towards their subordinates. This aim may be laudable in itself, but it is not by any means the whole story. We are suggesting that understanding nonverbal cues will help managers to gather information which will help them to be more *effective* managers. In fact, there is evidence that people with a more task-oriented style of leadership tend to be better at decoding nonverbal cues than people with a more socioemotional style of leadership.[25]

However, two factors must be taken into account when considering the application of research into nonverbal behaviour in practical situations. Firstly, the research is largely based upon the responses of American and British middle class subjects. Some nonverbal cues, like the facial expression of emotion, seem to be constant across cultures, but others are not. One example is the question of eye contact which we discussed earlier. It has been found that black and white Americans differ in the amount of time each spends looking at another person whilst talking or listening to them. In general, whites tend to look at the other person more whilst listening and less whilst talking, whereas blacks look at the other person less whilst listening and more whilst talking. Thus, conversations between blacks and whites would be expected to produce situations where both looked at each other when the black was talking and both looked away when the white was talking. Such situations could readily produce serious misinterpretation of nonverbal cues. The white speaker's lack of eye contact whilst talking could appear shifty or nervous to the black listener, whereas the black listener's lack of eye contact could be seen as lack of attention or sullenness. Conversely the black speaker's high eye contact could be seen as overbearing or insistent to the white listener and the white listener's high eye contact could be seen as insubordinate or hostile by the black speaker.[26] Such research shows clearly the dangers of assuming that all the nonverbal cues employed by different groups necessarily have the same meaning.

Secondly, there is the question of how skills in expressing and interpreting nonverbal cues are to be developed. Skills are learned through practice with feedback. Unfortunately, the opportunity to obtain feedback concerning nonverbal skills is much more limited than it is with verbal communication. If one passes the salt instead of the pepper because one has misinterpreted a verbal cue, one is likely to receive explicit feedback, "No I wanted the pepper." If, however, one misinterprets a nonverbal signal, an explicit verbal correction is less likely to occur. Indeed, there is research evidence that there is virtually no relationship between self ratings of decoding skills and actual ability to decode nonverbal cues. A positive relationship has been found between peoples' rating of their ability to express nonverbal cues and their actual ability to do so. DePaulo and Rosenthal[27] suggest that feedback may be an important factor here. When we express ourselves emotionally, we receive more immediate and more obtrusive feedback than when we read the emotional expressions of others. Even so, it is probably much easier to monitor what one is saying, and if necessary correct it, than it is to monitor and correct the *way* one is saying it, e.g. tone of voice, body posture, etc. It is one thing to realize that the way one has said something has not had the effect one would have liked, but quite another to know precisely what one should do to put it right. The question of feedback in the aquisition of nonverbal skills will be taken up again in Chapter 8.

REFERENCES

1   A Mehrabian (1971), *Silent Messages*, Wadsworth.

2   JA Edinger and ML Patterson (1983), 'Nonverbal Involvement and Social Control', *Psychological Bulletin*, Vol. 93, pp. 30–56.

3   For a detailed review of research in this area, see AW Siegman and S Feldstein (eds) (1978), *Nonverbal Behaviour and Communication*, Erlbaum/Wiley, particularly Chapters 3 and 7.

4   P Ekman (1978), 'Facial Expression' in Siegman and Feldstein, *op.cit.*

5   AT Dittman (1978), 'The Role of Body Movement in Communication', in Siegman and Feldstein, *op.cit.*

6   Dittman (1978), *op.cit.*

7   Ekman (1978), *op.cit.*

8   JR Davitz (1964), *The Communication of Emotional Meaning*, McGraw-Hill.
    W Apple and K Hecht (1982), 'Speaking Emotionally: The Relation Between Verbal and Vocal Communication of Affect', *Journal of Personality and Social Psychology*, Vol. 42, pp. 864–875.

9   KL Burns and EG Beier (1973), 'Significance of Vocal and Visual Channels in the Decoding of Emotional Meaning', *Journal of Communication*, Vol. 23, pp. 118–30.

10 AW Siegman (1978), 'Nonverbal messages of verbal communication', in Siegman and Feldstein, *op.cit.*

11 Dittman (1978), *op.cit.*
    RV Exline and BJ Fehr (1978), 'Applications of Semiosis to the Study of Visual Interaction', in Siegman and Feldstein, *op.cit.*

12 ML Patterson (1978), 'The Role of Space in Social Interaction' in Siegman and Feldstein, *op.cit.*

13 RV Exline, SL Ellyson and B Long (1975), 'Visual Behaviour as an Aspect of Power Role Relationships', in P Pilner, L Krames and T Alloway (eds), *Advances in the Study of Communication and Affect* (Vol 2), Plenum Press.

14 JF Dovidio and SL Ellyson (1982), 'Decoding Visual Dominance: Attributions of Power Based on Relative Percentages of Looking While Speaking and Looking While Listening', *Social Psychology Quarterly*, Vol. 45, pp. 106–113.

15 B Pope and AW Siegman (1972), 'Relationship and Verbal Behaviour in the Initial Interview', in AW Siegman and B Pope (eds), *Studies in Dyadic Communication*, Pergamon Press.

16 BM DePaulo and R Rosenthal (1979), Ambivalence, Discrepancy and Deception in Nonverbal Communication', in R Rosenthal (ed), *Skill in Nonverbal Communication*, Oelgeschlager, Gunn and Hain.

17 R Sommer (1965), 'Further Studies in Small Group Ecology', *Sociometry*, Vol. 28, pp. 337–348.
    M Cook (1970), 'Experiments on Orientation and Proxemics', *Human Relations*, Vol. 23, pp. 61–76.

18 P Ekman and WV Friesen (1969), 'The Repertoire of Nonverbal Behaviour: Categories, Origins, Usage and Coding', *Semiotica*, Vol. 1, pp. 49–98.

19 HM Rosenfeld (1978), 'Conversational Control Functions', in Siegman and Feldstein, *op.cit.*

20 Rosenfeld (1978), *op.cit.*

21 Rosenfeld (1978), *op.cit.*

22 Exline and Fehr (1978), *op.cit.*
Siegman (1978), *op.cit.*

23 JA Hall (1979), 'Gender, Gender Roles, and Nonverbal Communication Skills', in R. Rosenthal (ed), *Skill in Nonverbal Communication*, Oelgeschlager, Gunn and Hain.

24 Patterson (1978), *op.cit.*

25 Hall (1979), *op.cit.*

26 M LaFrance and C Mayo (1976), 'Racial Differences in Gaze Behaviour During Conversations', *Journal of Personality and Social Psychology*, Vol 33, pp. 547–552.

27 DePaulo and Rosenthal (1979), *op.cit.*

Chapter 6

Structuring Interactions with Subordinates

INTRODUCTION

In short interactions with subordinates, the questions and statements described in Chapter 4 may be used singly. For example, a closed question may elicit the precise piece of information required or an order may be obeyed instantly, without any further interaction being necessary. Usually, however, manager–subordinate interactions are more complex than such simple one-component exchanges. Even if the manager simply says "Thank you" on receiving the information or when the subordinate signals compliance, then two components are being used in sequence, closed question then recognition, or order than recognition, and we can see the beginnings of an interaction structure. In longer interactions, the discussion may cover several different topics, each of which consists of a number of different components, sequenced in different ways.

This provides us with two ways of looking at the structure of manager–subordinate interactions. There is the way in which particular components follow each other in sequence and, in longer interactions, the way in which the interaction as a whole, and the topics covered within it, are introduced, sequenced, resolved and so on.

SEQUENCES OF COMPONENTS

We will examine sequences of components first. Consider the following examples:

Manager: "I see from the latest production figures that output was down last month. Do you have any ideas why that should be?" **Open question**

Subordinate: "Well we had some problems with absenteeism, but I think the main problem was machine breakdown."

Manager: "That was a serious problem last month?" **Restatement**

Subordinate: "Yes, we would have easily reached production targets if it hadn't been for that."

Manager:	"How many hours did we lose altogether?"	**Closed question**
Subordinate:	"About five or six hours. I don't have the exact figures with me, but about that."	
Manager:	"Was it the same machine or different ones?"	**Comparison**
Subordinate:	"The same one. The new automatic baler."	
Manager:	"Is there any particular reason why that one should be causing problems?	**Probe**
Subordinate:	"Not really. It's an excellent machine. We tested it thoroughly before we bought it . . . There is one thing though . . .	
Manager:	"Mmmm . . ."	**Lubricant**
Subordinate:	"Well if the automatic baler breaks down, the whole department grinds to a halt, and everyone has to wait until it's repaired. With the others, we can shift people around and keep production going, but with the automatic baler, everyone gets a break."	
Manager:	"So you think it might be the operators?"	**Closed question**
Subordinate:	"Well I can't prove it, but I'm beginning to think it might be."	
Manager:	"Well that is certainly something which needs to be looked into. Over the next month I think you should keep a close eye on that machine. Check whether there is any sabotage or whether there is any other reason why that particular machine should cause us problems. Let me know what you find at the next production meeting, or earlier if you come up with something significant."	**Order**
Subordinate:	"Right, I'll do that."	
Manager:	"OK, that's one reason for the fall off in output.	**Bridge**
	Any others? You said something earlier about absenteeism . . .	**Open**

Another manager might tackle the same problem as follows:

Manager:	"I see from the latest production figures that output was down last month. You realize how serious this is, don't you?"	**Leading question**
Subordinate:	"Well yes, I do. I'm always conscious of . . .	

Manager:	"So what are you going to do about it?"	**Probe**
Subordinate:	"Well, I'm keeping a close eye on things. One of the problems we've had is with machine breakdown. We lost a lot of time through machine breakdown last month."	
Manager:	"That shouldn't happen. With proper maintenance schedules, those machines should run virtually non-stop. You do realize how important proper maintenance is, don't you?"	**Leading question**
Subordinate:	"Yes, I . . ."	
Manager:	"And you are keeping to the official maintenance procedures, I take it?"	**Leading question**
Subordinate:	"Oh yes, definitely."	
Manager:	"Good. Well I want you to keep a particularly close eye on these machines over the next month. Check each machine thoroughly and make sure that correct maintenance procedures are being followed. And I'll expect a big improvement next week, all right.	**Order**
Subordinate:	(Dubiously) "Yes, all right, I'll do that . . . but there is one other thing . . .	
Manager:	"Good. And another thing. Absenteeism was high again last month. You can't expect to run an efficient department when half your staff don't turn up, can you?"	**Leading question**

These two examples illustrate a number of factors which may influence what is achieved in such interactions between managers and subordinates.

1. The Components Employed

The first example illustrates the use of a variety of components—probes, comparison questions, closed questions—in order to elicit more precise information after an initial open question. The open question allowed the subordinate to state what he thought was the most important problem in general terms, whilst each successive question brings the manager closer to the key problem until it is finally identified. The key point is that the manager did not know what this key problem was before the introduction started, and therefore this sequence was necessary in order to discover the key question he or she should ask. In an ideal world, of course, the subordinate would immediately realize what was the key information the manager required and volunteer it straight away, rendering the use of skilful questionning unnecessary. In the real world, however, subordinates are often, rightly or wrongly, reluctant to give their bosses the particular piece of information which might be useful to them. It might be because they do not realize that it would be useful, or because they are afraid it will be used against them, or, as in this case, because the subordinate is not yet sufficiently sure of his or her facts. In such cases, skilful questionning techniques may be essential to gain the information required.

In the second example an inappropriate sequence of components is used leading to a much less satisfactory conclusion. There is little variety in components used. The continual use of leading questions results in the manager simply confirming his or her own prejudices rather than learning anything new. One probing question is used, which could in another context be useful. Here, however, it is sprung on the subordinate suddenly, without giving him the opportunity to get his thoughts together and the information obtained was less useful than it might have been.

2. Pace of the Interaction

One factor which influences the quality of information gathered and the quality of decisions made is the pace of the interaction. By this we mean not only the speed with which manager and/or subordinate speak, but also, and more crucially, the speed with which their respective contributions follow each other. In the second example, the manager on several occasions did not allow the subordinate to finish his response before asking another question or introducing another topic. Excessive pace in an interaction has a number of adverse effects:

- It denies the subordinate time to give a reasoned, relevant reply
- It denies the manager time to understand the implications of what the subordinate is saying
- It denies the manager time to phrase the right question or statement which will produce the response he or she requires.

Managers are, of course, very busy most of the time. Mintzberg[1] for example, talks of "much work at unrelenting pace." Paradoxically, however, a slower pace of interaction may achieve the same or better results more quickly. The shorter the time available, the more essential it is not to waste time by asking irrelevant questions or making irrelevant statements which do not achieve the most beneficial results. It may take longer to select just the right question, but it is more likely to solve the problem and do so in less time than six rapid-fire but inappropriate ones.

A number of devices can be used to slow an interaction down to provide thinking time:

(a) *Allow Silence* Many people seem to find silence disturbing. They cannot think precisely what they should say next, so rather than say nothing, they say the first thing which comes into their head, which may not further the aims of the interaction at all. On the other hand, silence need not be embarrassing, providing the person using it is doing so purposefully. In this case, it is not a sign of inadequacy, but the skilful use of time to achieve a more desirable outcome. It can, however, then become even more disturbing to the other person, particularly if they have just said something tendentious or asked a pointed question. The ensuing silence may then put pressure on him or her to say something, either modifying or elaborating on what he or she has just said.

(b) Labelling If silence would cause unwanted tension in the interaction, this can be avoided by verbalizing what is happening. The manager can quite simply say "Wait a minute, let's think about this for a moment", or some similar phrase. Having overtly labelled the silence as a pause for thought seems to make it much less threatening to both parties.

(c) Restatement Another useful device for obtaining thinking time providing it is not overused, is to restate or paraphrase what the other person has just said. This throws the conversational ball back into the other person's court, and whilst he or she is talking, elaborating on the original statement, the manager can be thinking of his or her next attack on the question. An example occurs in the first example, where the manager says with respect to the subordinate's comment about machine breakdown: "That was a serious problem last month?" Used appropriately, such restatements can also signal that the manager is listening or act as an open question signifying "Tell me more about that." They are not, however, infallible—the subordinate may simply reply "Yes"—and would become very tedious if overused.

3. Listening

An important influence on the structure of and outcomes from an interaction is the extent to which the manager actually listens to what the subordinate is saying. This applies both to the words themselves and to nonverbal cues of enthusiasm, doubt, acceptance and rejection, etc. which are conveyed by tone of voice, pace of speaking, and so on. Visual cues such as posture and facial expression, are also important indicators of the other person's feelings. Just as it is important for the manager to convey the same message by means of verbal and nonverbal cues if he or she is to be convincing, a lack of correspondence between verbal and nonverbal cues on the part of the subordinate is a sign that he or she is not convinced, and further discussion is necessary.

Several instances of listening and not listening are included in the examples. As noted above, the first manager's use of repetition—if used with appropriate nonverbal cues—is a sign that he or she is listening, as is the use of lubricators later and the reintroduction of absenteeism into the discussion after the subordinates earlier comment. In the second example, the manager does not 'hear' the subordinate's doubts about routine maintenance being the solution to the problem and continually interrupts thus depriving him or herself of the opportunity to listen. Both manager and subordinate had 'another thing' they wanted to talk about at the end of the extract. However, the manager did not give the subordinate an opportunity to express this point, and it may have been important.

Acquiring listening skills is a difficult task. It is not a question of developing a few simple techniques, but of changing ones whole approach to an interaction. This is discussed in more detail in the next chapter. However, it is worth noting here that for training purposes an audio or audio visual replay of an incident of non-listening on the part of the trainee is a very useful way of demonstrating the need for the development of listening skills. At the end of the interaction, the second manager would probably be convinced that the subordinate had accepted the need for more careful routine maintenance. If he listened to a replay, concentrating only on the extent of the subordinate's acceptance of the idea, the subordinate's doubts would probably be immediately apparent.

4. Reaching a Conclusion

Although the two interactions described at the beginning of this chapter differ in a number of ways, they do have one thing in common. Both reach a conclusion. The conclusion may be less relevant in the second example because of the manager's inferior questioning and listening skills, but nevertheless the subordinate does clearly understand what the manager thinks he should do next. In some cases, however, the opposite problem may arise. The manager may skilfully collect the information required and then fail to use it in order to come to a conclusion which fulfils the purpose of the interaction.

This is not to say that *all* interactions between managers and subordinates should have an apparent purpose. As this is a book on leadership skills, we are concentrating on those which do. However, some interactions may take place simply for the enjoyment of the interaction itself, e.g. a discussion of a recent football match or an amusing incident which took place in another department. This is not to say that such interactions may not have a useful function—they will probably engender a closer working relationship between the manager and subordinate—but unless the manager is particularly socially inept, such interactions will probably be more successful if allowed to happen spontaneously rather than consciously planned.

On the other hand, work interactions, almost by definition, do have a purpose, and can be counted as failures to the extent that it is not achieved. Three main purposes of work interaction can be identified, which parallel the types of components described in Chapter 4.

(a) Allowing the Subordinate To Let Off Steam

Here the purpose is to allow the subordinate to give vent to some emotion which he or she wants to express. It might be a sense of grievance or resentment or enthusiasm or triumph. If the manager wishes to encourage this, because it will reduce dissatisfaction or enhance motivation, then lubricators, restatements, reflectives (e.g. "You must have been upset about that" or "I'll bet you felt great") and a great deal of active listening will be very useful. The interaction will have achieved its primary purpose when the subordinate signals that he or she has now returned to a more even emotional state (e.g. "I'm glad I got all that off my chest; I feel a lot better for it"). It may be that, in the course of the discussion, information emerged which suggested further action could be taken to prevent a grievance happening again or capitalize on a success. If the subordinate's emotions are running very high it is probably better to ignore these possible actions until the emotions have dissipated, and then take them up.

(b) Gathering Information

In some interactions, the manager may simply want to obtain information from the subordinate. It may be information about the subordinate, e.g. whether family circumstances would permit easy relocation should the opportunity of a transfer arise. Alternatively, it may be information which the manager requires to make a decision about other matters which do not involve any future action on the part of the subordinate, e.g. performance data concerning a new machine in order to decide whether it should be introduced in other departments. The interaction can be said to have successfully achieved its purpose when the manager has collected all the information which the subordinate can contribute towards making a good decision. If the manager fails to do this, then he or she can, of course, re-open the discussion at a later date and ask further questions. However, this is time consuming, and may also be irritating or even undiplomatic. The question of availability for transfer raised once could be casual interest, but raised twice might cause unwanted speculation and uncertainty. It is often, therefore, more effective and certainly more elegant to get all the information first time. If the issue is sufficiently important or delicate, therefore, it could be worthwhile identifying the key information required to make a good decision before the interaction commences and asking oneself before closing the discussion: "Do I have sufficient information to make a good decision now?" If the answer is no, then more probes, open questions, and so on are called for.

(c) Influencing Behaviour

Finally, the purpose of the interaction may be to take actions in order to improve the subordinate's work performance, and may be taken by the subordinate, the manager or both. For example, the manager might conclude: "Over the next four weeks I want you to check the maintenance records of the automatic baler to see whether there is any pattern and keep a close eye on its current performance. In the meantime, I will check with our other factories to see whether they have had any problems with the same machine."

As we noted earlier, a manager may fail to arrive at a high quality solution because he or she has failed to collect the relevant information. Equally, however, managers may skilfully collect the information but fail to use it to reach a clear cut conclusion. Such interactions not only leave problems unsolved, but are also likely to leave the subordinate with the feelings that interactions with the manager are a waste of time because they never achieve anything.

It is a useful exercise, therefore, to conclude the discussion of each problem area with a summary of what is to be done about it. Of course, it would be naive to assume that all problems *can* be solved, but even failure to solve a problem is worth summarizing to establish between manager and subordinate exactly where they have got to and what is to be done next, e.g. shelve it until a later meeting, refer it elsewhere, collect more information, or bring someone else into the decision making process.

If it is difficult to find anything to summarize, then obviously the discussion has not come to an adequate conclusion. Furthermore, the discipline of making a summary will also focus the manager's mind during the preceding discussion, because he or she will realize that in order to be able to make an adequate summary, he or she will have to use the necessary interpersonal skills to arrive at an adequate solution in the first place.

One further concept is worth mentioning before we leave the question of sequences of components. So far we have been assuming that the decision about the next component to be used in a sequence is made spontaneously as the interaction progresses. In many cases this will be so. However, there also exist, whether by design or habit, sequences of components which typically follow the same pattern. This is akin to the driver who will have to make spontaneous responses to particular driving situations, but will also have a repertoire of habitual sequences of responses such as those involved in changing up the gears or making turns, and so on. In the context of manager–subordinate inter-actions, we have called such purposeful sequences of components *gambits*. Some are well known interviewing techniques discussed in the literature, others debating tricks, and still others perhaps merely habitual ways of interacting with other people which the manager has developed over the years and now uses without realizing. Some examples are:

The Funnel Technique

A gambit for homing in on some specific piece of information, in an area where a manager initially lacks sufficient background information to ask the precise question required. It consists of a very open question to begin with, followed by a narrowing series of probes. Thus the information gained from each question is used to phrase the next one more precisely, until the manager is able to ask for the specific piece of information required. The first example given at the beginning of this chapter broadly follows this pattern.

Hammering the Point Home

A gambit used to ensure that a subordinate has got the point. It consists of a series of orders, requests, pieces of advice or explanations, interspersed with leading questions, such as "you do understand don't you?" In other words, the manager ensures that a clear-cut conclusion is reached and understood by the subordinate by restating the same conclusion several times in different ways. Sometimes this may be necessary, but if the manager still continues once the subordinate has understood, then he or she is likely to become irritated and resentful. Thus correctly deciding the point at which to stop requires considerable skill, particularly in the interpretation of nonverbal cues.

Trap Setting
An attempt to get a subordinate to provide, without realizing it, information which will prove conclusively that he or she is wrong, made a mistake, or is at fault in some way. Commonly, it consists of a series of leading questions, eliciting compliant responses, until the trap is sprung with a triumphant leading criticism, such as "So, you admit that you simply weren't thinking when you . . ."

Causal Analysis
This is a gambit used by the authors to minimize the risk of emotional reactions to attempts to improve performance. It is a way of getting someone to recognize how he or she might do something better next time, without going through the stage of pointing out limitations in current performance, and in particular without using emotive words such as 'faults', 'shortcomings', 'went wrong', etc. Typically it consists of a series of open questions and probes, followed by recognition and/or advice, depending on the individual's ability to solve his or her own problems. For example:

"When you did X, what effect did that have?"

"Was that the effect you wanted to have?"

"What effect did you want to have?"

"In that case, can you think of any way you might have handled things differently to produce the result you wanted?"

"That's a good idea, why don't you try that next time?"

or

"And another way of tackling the problem would be to . . ."

or

"Well, one way of tackling the problem would be to . . ."

Obviously, such gambits will vary in their usefulness. Trap setting can be used once, or perhaps even twice, but thereafter, the interaction, and any subsequent interaction with the same subordinate, is likely to become extremely stilted as he or she examines each question for hidden implications. The others can undoubtedly be used much more often, but even they are likely to be counterproductive if used to excess, as the unvarying approach of the manager arouses suspicion, frustration or boredom. As with individual components, there is no one best way. The interpersonally skilled manager is one who, consciously or unconsciously has a wide variety of gambits at his or her disposal, and is able to select the one which is appropriate to his or her needs at a particular point in an interaction, but is also capable of droppiong it and trying another, or simply responding spontaneously to a subordinate's comments, should it not produce the desired result.

OVERALL STRUCTURE

We now turn to the longer interactions between manager and subordinate which may cover several issues within the same interaction. The question of structure arises here in relation to the way in which these issues are sequenced and related to each other, and the way the interaction as a whole is introduced and concluded. Consider the following interactions.

Example A

The manager (Ellen) calls her subordinate (Dan) into her office and tells him that she is concerned about his department's production figures for last month. She explains why she is concerned. There has been a complaint about late delivery, higher production figures have been achieved in the past, and she has had advance warning of a big sales drive which will require a stockpile of finished articles to meet the hoped-for dramatic increase in demand. She establishes that there are three main problem areas which have contributed in varying degrees to the lower production figures. These are machine breakdown, absenteeism and occasional shortage of raw materials. Each of these is discussed in turn, establishing precisely what the problem is, what its causes are and what can be done to prevent it happening again, or at least minimize its effects. Ellen then summarizes the agreed actions and both of them leave the meeting knowing exactly how they are going to tackle the problem.

Example B

The manager (Colin) calls his subordinate (George) into his office and tells him that he is concerned about his department's production figures. Colin begins by asking why so much time has been lost through machine breakdown and gathers some information on this question. He suggests that lack of routine maintenance may be the problem, but George argues that the main problem is absenteeism because this necessitates putting people on machines which they are not used to. The problem of absenteeism is discussed, but no clear cut conclusions reached. Colin then queries why production has been delayed by shortage of raw materials and George points out that forward planning is difficult because of the unpredictable nature of machine breakdowns. Colin returns to the question of routine maintenance, but George points out that recommended practices are already being followed. The discussion continues in this manner with the three main issues being raised and discussed, but dropped before any conclusion is reached. The meeting closes with Colin telling George that he will have to do something about falling production rates because there is a big sales push coming and they will need all the stocks they can build up. George agrees that something will have to be done, but leaves the meeting with no clear idea of what it is.

Example C

The Manager (Bill) calls his subordinate (Mary) into his office and tells her he is concerned about her department's production figures. Mary says she is very pleased to talk about the problem because she is worried too. Bill says that he has identified a number of things which he feels are contributory factors which he would like to discuss in turn, beginning with machine breakdown. Mary replies, with some emphasis, that her main problem is the supply of raw materials and, in particular, suppliers who do not keep to delivery dates no matter how many times they are reminded. She is told that they will come to that later, but firstly they will deal with machine breakdown. Mary replies that solving the machine breakdown problem will not make much difference if they do not have the raw materials anyway. Bill insists that they will get to the raw materials problem in good time, but first they will deal with the question of machine breakdown. For a moment they glare at each other in silence, but Mary then slumps in her chair and says: "OK, if that's the way you want it." For some time afterwards she makes little contribution to the discussion and is grudgingly acquiescent when Bill makes suggestions about what she should do to solve the machine breakdown and absenteeism problems. She brightens somewhat when the discussion finally gets round to the raw material problem and makes a number of useful contributions. Bill summarizes what they have agreed and Mary leaves the meeting in a somewhat happier frame of mind than she was after the first five minutes, when she was within an inch of telling him what he could do with his job and his machines. However, she is by no means convinced that Bill's suggestions on the machine breakdown and absenteeism problems will have any useful effect at all.

These examples illustrate some of the advantages and disadvantages of different ways of structuring manager–subordinate interactions. These interactions vary in the extent to which the manager establishes an *organized* structure for the interaction. Any organized structure, as we would define it, is one which consists of a logical sequence of discrete sections, each of which deals with a single major topic. Ideally, each section will reach an agreed conclusion, and the topic will not be raised again until the final summary. If this happens, then the final summary should be relatively straightforward, simply a repetition of the points agreed at the end of each section to remind both manager and subordinate of the main conclusions they have reached. If full agreement has not been established earlier, then disagreements are likely to arise at the summary stage, extending the interaction, perhaps causing friction, and certainly reducing the clarity of the conclusions. Example A is an illustration of a successful interaction using an organized structure.

At the opposite extreme is Example B, which is an interaction with a *diffuse* structure. That is, one in which the topics covered take the form of a number of themes, which occur and reoccur throughout the interaction, interwoven with each other. There are situations where such a structure might be effective. For example, if the manager is trying to defuse a highly charged emotional situation by allowing the subordinate to talk him or herself out, then the manager will simply respond (with reflectives, restatements and lubricators) to the subordinate's comments rather than attempt to impose his or her own structure on to the interaction. For most purposes, however, a diffuse structure is likely to suffer the major drawback that each issue is dropped before agreement is reached about how the problem is to be tackled. Each time it is raised again involves some going over old ground, thus the end result is often a long interaction with no clear cut conclusions.

An interaction structure can either be developed during or before an interaction. If there is not time to plan the interaction beforehand or the manager does not know all the ramifications of the problem to be discussed then the structure can be developed at the beginning of the interaction. For example, the interaction might begin in the following way.

Example D

Manager:	"As you know, I'm worried about the recent fall in output in your department, Dan, and I think we should work out a joint plan of campaign to deal with the problem."
Subordinate:	"OK"
Manager:	"Now, there are two major contributory factors I can identify—machine breakdown and raw material supply. I think we need to have a very close look at both these questions. Is there any other factor which you would identify?"
Subordinate:	"Absenteeism. That's a big problem."
Manager:	"Anything else?"
Subordinate:	"No, I think those are the main three."
Manager:	"Very well, we'll deal with each in turn. Where would you like to start?"
Subordinate:	"Absenteeism. That's my biggest headache."
Manager:	"OK, we'll start with that and then go on to machine breakdown and raw materials supply. So, tell me about the problems you've been having with absenteeism."

If the manager knows beforehand that an interaction is to take place on some particular topic, and the topic is important enough to warrant it, then advance planning can be very useful. The plan might consist of a list of the major topics the manager wishes to raise, the key points to be raised within each topic, and some hypotheses concerning possible outcomes or conclusions of the interaction. The manager equipped with such a plan will be in a much better position to select and perform individual components of the interaction skilfully than one who is at the same time attempting to structure the interaction as a whole.

Whilst a plan may be useful, however, rigid adherence to it can be disastrous. Even the most well thought-out plan may turn out to be inappropriate because of something which happens in the course of the discussion. It may be that the subordinate finds some particular issue extremely sensitive and is obviously very uneasy about discussing it further. The manager will then have to decide whether more is to be gained by proceeding with the issue there and then or leaving it until some later occasion when both have had time to think it over. Similarly, the subordinate may have some burning issue which is preventing him or her from concentrating on other things until it is cleared up. Again, the manager will have to decide whether more is to be gained by sticking to the original plan or changing it to accommodate the subordinate's priorities. Much will depend upon how relevant is the issue which the subordinate wishes to discuss, how flexible the subordinate is and how important he or she feels the issue is. If it is simply a matter of changing the order in which issues are discussed, then there is a strong argument for doing so. A subordinate who is highly concerned about one particular topic may simply 'switch off' until it is dealt with and the value of much of the earlier discussion will be lost. Example C is an illustration of what can happen when a plan is too rigidly adhered to in the face of changing circumstances. Nevertheless, a plan can still be useful even if it is changed by force of circumstance. It can be used as a checklist—the manager can cross off the items as they are dealt with, and a glance at the list will show those issues still remaining. The manager can then restructure the remainder of the interaction much more easily than would be possible if he or she had no plan at all.

A similar point is made by Rackham and Carlisle[2] in their study of the factors involved in effective negotiation. They found that less successful or 'average' negotiators placed heavy reliance on *sequence planning*. That is, their plans were based on the assumption that they would discuss a number of issues in a certain order, each linked with and leading to the next. They would frequently verbalize a potential negotiation in terms like "First I'll bring up A, then lead to B, and after that I'll cover C and finally go on to D." Rackham and Carlisle point out that in order to succeed, sequence planning requires the consent and cooperation of the other party to the negotiation, and often this is not forthcoming. By contrast, successful negotiators were more likely to use *issue planning*. That is, they tended to plan around each individual issue in a way which was independent of any sequence, and were careful not to draw sequence links between issues.

One further point is worth making about the way in which manager–subordinate interactions are structured. The structure used need not bear any relationship to the manager's leadership style. A manager using an organized structure could be democratic or participative, in that he or she allows the subordinate a large say in defining the structure (as in Example D). Alternatively, the manager may develop his or her own structure and impose this on the subordinate irrespective of his or her wishes (as in Example C). Similarly, a manager using a diffuse structure may be democratically deferring to the subordinate's wishes or autocratically criticizing the subordinate on a number of unrelated issues as they come to mind. Given that it is possible to perform the same style in such radically different ways, it is hardly surprising that the research literature provides little evidence of any consistent relationship between leadership styles and performance (Korman[3], Stogdill[4]).

REFERENCES

1   H Mintzberg (1980), *The Nature of Managerial Work*, Prentice-Hall.

2   N Rackham and J Carlisle (1978), 'The Effective Negotiator Part 2: Planning for Negotiations', *J. European Industrial Training*, Vol. 2, No. 7, pp. 2–5.

3   AK Korman (1966), ' "Consideration", "Initiating Structure", and Organizational Criteria. A Review', *Personnel Psychology*, Vol. 21, No. 4, pp. 349–361.

4   RM Stogdill (1974), *Handbook of Leadership: A Survey of Theory and Research*, Free Press.

Chapter 7

Approaches to Manager–Subordinate Interactions

INTRODUCTION

In previous chapters we have described the range of verbal and nonverbal components which a manager can use in an interaction with a subordinate, and the different ways in which such interactions can be structured. However, it is extremely unlikely that a manager will use all these in any one interaction. Those actually used will depend in part upon the reactions of the subordinate. For example, the subordinate may provide information readily or be evasive, respond willingly to attempts to influence his or her behaviour or resist them, become angry, enthusiastic or apathetic, and so on. This will, in turn, influence what the manager says and does to a greater or lesser degree. This can vary from simply asking a question another way or restating an order more firmly to restructuring the whole interaction because the subordinate is not responding as expected.

However, another influence on the components used in an interaction and the way it is structured is the manager's preference with respect to the kind of interaction he or she wishes to have with the subordinate. Two factors are important here. One is the extent to which the manager is prepared to allow the subordinate to influence the content of the interaction and the decisions which are reached. The other is the extent to which the manager wishes to conduct the interaction in a warm, friendly manner or one which is cold and businesslike, emphasizing differences in status and authority. Both these will influence the manager's general approach to the interaction and therefore the verbal and nonverbal components and ways of structuring the interaction which he or she chooses to use. As noted in Chapter 1, this aspect of leadership has been the major concern of theorists for many years. Much has been written about the relative merits of the democratic, autocratic, participative, authoritarian, person-centred, task oriented, considerate, and many other similar leadership styles. Nevertheless, this type of theory has a major drawback from our point of view: it does not describe in any detail how to perform these various leadership styles or what skills are needed to perform them well. Norman Maier[1] has, however, addressed this problem, not as a leadership theorist, but in relation to performance appraisal interviewing.

Maier suggests that there are three types of appraisal interview, which he calls the 'Tell and Sell', the 'Tell and Listen' and the 'Problem Solving'. Essentially, these are different methods of giving subordinates feedback about past performance and/or establishing plans for future performance improvement. Maier makes the important point that successful appraisal interviewing depends on both selecting the right method *and* on having the necessary skills. However, Maier does not claim that any one type of interview is superior to the others in all circumstances. Rather, he suggests that each method has its own advantages and limitations, depending on the objectives the manager wishes to achieve, the employee's age and experience, the way in which the employee is likely to react to the approach, and so on. Maier, therefore, not only describes each type of appraisal interview, but also indicates the skills which will be required to perform them successfully, and the circumstances in which their use would be appropriate and inappropriate.

Furthermore, the use of Maier's three approaches need not be restricted to the formal appraisal interview; they could equally well be used as general techniques for the day-to-day management of staff. We therefore decided to take Maier's work on appraisal interviewing, rather than leadership theory, as the starting point for our analysis of the different ways in which managers can approach interactions with their subordinates. As might be expected, however, it required some further development in a number of areas before it could provide a comprehensive framework for the analysis of leadership skills at this level.

PURPOSE OF THE INTERACTION

Because they were described within the context of appraisal interviewing Maier's three approaches were originally envisaged as means of providing feedback about past performance and establishing plans for performance improvement.

However, interactions which take place in the course of day-to-day management may also have several other purposes. The manager is likely to have a wide variety of information, apart from feedback about performance, which could help the subordinate to do his or her job more effectively. Similarly, the manager will have a wide variety of other problems, apart from the subordinate's work performance, with which the subordinate may be able to help, either by providing relevant information or suggesting alternative solutions. Conversely, the subordinate may ask for the manager's help in solving a personal problem or demand action to resolve a grievance. Whilst Maier's three approaches were not originally intended for such purposes it would be possible to use one or more of them in each of these types of interaction. However, this would require considerable broadening of their scope. Furthermore, they may not represent the most appropriate approach in all circumstances.

RANGE OF APPROACHES AND ASSOCIATED COMPONENTS

Maier describes only three types of appraisal interview; however, it is possible to identify three other approaches which could be used either in appraisals or in other interactions between manager and subordinate. These others we call the 'Tell', the 'Ask and Tell' and 'Ask and Listen'. Moreover, Maier indicates only in very general terms the skills required for his approaches. For example, the Tell and Listen approach requires the skills of active listening, use of pauses, and reflecting and summarizing feelings, but he does not describe in any detail the questions and statements the manager would need either to influence behaviour or gather information. We feel that for purposes of skill development it is important to draw out such links between different approaches and the components which are required for their effective use. Our full list of approaches and their associated components is therefore as follows.

The Tell Approach

Using the Tell approach the manager simply informs the subordinate of his or her decision, without first asking the subordinate for his or her opinions and without giving any specific reasons, arguments or other inducements for accepting it. The obvious component of this approach is the order, but requests, suggestions or advice may also be used, e.g. "I must ask you to . . ." or "I would strongly advise you not to . . .".

The successful use of the Tell approach relies heavily on the manager's ability to make correct decisions without checking them out with the subordinate, and the subordinate's willingness to accept these decisions without question. Under certain conditions both these requirements may be fulfilled:

- when the decision is simple, and the solution self evident
- when the manager is an expert, and respected as such by the subordinate
- when there is an emergency, and the subordinate recognizes that there is no time for detailed discussion or explanation.

The manager can also increase the probability of having made the right decision in the first place by thoroughly checking his or her facts and examining alternative interpretations or solutions.

Conditions which are likely to increase the acceptability of the Tell approach to the subordinate (but not necessarily the validity of the decision) include:

- an organizational climate in which giving orders is an accepted norm, e.g. the armed forces and emergency services
- compliant subordinates who accept or prefer an authoritarian style
- where the manager has high reward and/or punishment power, and is known to use this to reinforce his or her decisions
- where the manager has much higher status in the organization than the subordinate.

The main advantage of the Tell approach is that it saves time when rapid decisions have to be made. It can also be useful when other methods of behavioural influence have been used and resulted in irreconcilable differences of opinion. If the manager is convinced that his or her viewpoint is correct, then the Tell approach can be used to curtail further fruitless argument. In some cases, it may even be preferable to the subordinate to have an issue settled in this way, particularly if he or she has come to the conclusion that further discussion would be a waste of time because it would inevitably lead to the same decision whatever arguments were put forward.

The Tell approach may also appear to be a very convenient general technique for the management of people. It saves managers all the time and effort required to explain their decisions to their subordinates, find out what motivates them, examine alternative viewpoints, and so on. Nevertheless, for most purposes, the Tell approach has a number of serious drawbacks. Subordinates who do not know why they are doing something are much less able to react adaptively to unforeseen circumstances. Many will be less motivated to perform well if they do not understand the reasons for what they are doing. They may resent the manager simply telling them what to do, and either object openly or respond with reluctant compliance. Finally, the subordinates may have useful information or alternative suggestions which could have helped the manager to make a better decision in the first place.

Furthermore, we suspect that it may be very tempting to underestimate the importance of these factors. It would be pleasant indeed to believe that we can reach good decisions without needing help from other people, particularly subordinates, and that our subordinates hold us in such respect that they would be only too willing to implement our decisions without question. Unfortunately, being sure that one is right is no guarantee that one actually is, or that one's subordinates will be equally convinced. As a result, decisions reached using the Tell approach can be of poor quality, grudgingly implemented and sometimes deliberately sabotaged. Except in an emergency or as a last resort, therefore, it is usually more effective to use one of the other approaches.

The Tell and Sell Approach

Using the Tell and Sell approach, the manager informs the subordinate of his or her decision, and then attempts to persuade the subordinate to accept it by pointing out its advantages, personal or organizational. Typically, this approach involves the use of orders, requests, advice or suggestions, followed by explanations, threats or promises. Other components commonly used are leading questions, praise, criticism, inhibitors and summaries. Leading questions are used in an attempt to get the subordinate to express overt acceptance of the manager's viewpoint, and praise to get the subordinate in a good mood and more prepared to listen to the manager. Criticism is used to bring home to subordinates their responsibility for past failures and the need for future performance improvement. In a well organized Tell and Sell, summaries will be used to draw together and emphasize the main points which the manager wishes to put across. The subordinate's role in all this is intended to be relatively passive: listening attentively to what the manager has to say and then agreeing, preferably enthusiastically. If the subordinate attempts to contribute more, therefore, inhibitors are likely to be used in an attempt to prevent the subordinate from speaking and allow the manager to retain the speaking role. Finally, the gambit 'hammering the point home' may also be used as part of the Tell and Sell approach.

The main advantage of the Tell and Sell approach is that it can be brief and to the point, getting a relatively simple message across clearly and unequivocally. It can be useful with relatively inexperienced members of staff who have not yet had time to develop ideas of their own or with subordinates who prefer to be told, rather than be involved in participative decision-making. It is also the most appropriate approach for disciplinary interviews, where both the required improvement in performance and the consequences of not achieving it within a certain time, need to be spelled out in detail.

Like the Tell approach, the effective use of Tell and Sell relies upon the ability of the manager to make the right decision in the first place. However, with the Tell and Sell, the manager must also be sure that the subordinate will 'buy' whatever is being sold. This requires a good understanding of human motivation in general and also the needs of the subordinate in question. Being able to identify such inducements and tying their attainment to acceptance of the decision can result in a highly motivated subordinate who knows precisely what he or she is expected to do.

Used inappropriately, however, the approach has two main limitations. Firstly, it inhibits independent judgement. The subordinate may have a useful contribution to make to the matter being discussed and this will not emerge as long as the manager adheres to a Tell and Sell approach. Furthermore, allowing the subordinate to put forward his or her ideas, whether or not these are finally accepted, provides the manager with an opportunity to assess the subordinate's knowledge and judgement, and develop the subordinate's decision-making skills by giving feedback and guidance, evaluating alternative suggestions, etc. Secondly, the Tell and Sell approach may not have the intended motivational effect with all subordinates. Some may simply not like to be told. Others may not like what they are told on a particular occasion, the way they are told it, or they may be indifferent to the inducements. If the manager persists with the Tell and Sell approach under these circumstances, it is likely to be counterproductive. Some subordinates may express disagreement overtly, resulting in a time-consuming and perhaps acrimonious argument. Others may hide their disagreement and overtly accept the manager's decision, knowing that this is the quickest way of escaping from a potentially unpleasant situation. However, because they have no commitment to the decision, it will be implemented with little enthusiasm if at all. Worse still, if the manager is poor at reading nonverbal cues, he or she may not even realize that the interaction has failed to attain its intended objectives.

Tell and Listen

Using the Tell and Listen approach, the manager informs the subordinate of his or her decision, and then asks the subordinate for his or her views about it. Like the Tell and Sell approach, the manager typically begins the interaction using orders, requests, advice or suggestions, perhaps combined with praise and criticism, but then in the Listen phase employs information-gathering components such as open questions, comparisons, hypotheticals, lubricators, and so on. Among the gambits, 'hammering the point home' may be used in the Tell phase and 'trap setting' during the Listen phase.

The advantage of this approach is that it can lead to decreased defensiveness and high levels of motivation on the part of some subordinates, because they feel that their views have been taken into account. If the subordinates do express their views honestly, and this depends largely upon the manager's manner, the manager will not leave the interaction with a false impression of the subordinate's commitment. Furthermore, if the manager actually does take the subordinate's views into account, this may allow a better decision to be reached than if the manager took the decision on his or her own.

On the other hand, unless the outcomes of the interaction are well summarized at the end, there is a danger that their impact may be dissipated during the Listen phase. Thus the interaction may produce no clear cut conclusions. There is also a danger that the subordinates may produce information or alternative suggestions during the Listen phase which totally invalidates what they have been told earlier, rendering the Tell phase a complete waste of time. Finally, past experience may tell the subordinate that the manager never really listens or becomes annoyed if disagreement is expressed. Thus the subordinate may simply agree from expediency, leaving the manager with the false impression that his or her views have been accepted.

Ask and Tell

Using the Ask and Tell approach, the manager first obtains information from the subordinate concerning some problem area and then tells the subordinate what he or she has decided. Thus the approach involves the initial use of information-gathering components, such as open questions, probes, hypotheticals, lubricators, restatements, etc. followed by orders, requests, advice, suggestions or leading questions and perhaps also threats and promises in order to 'sell' the decision. Gambits such as the 'funnel technique', 'trap setting' and 'hammering the point home' may also be used.

This approach has several advantages. Firstly, the information obtained from the subordinate during the Ask phase may enable the manager to reach a better decision than could otherwise have been achieved. The key to the approach is the fact that the manager gathers this information before revealing his or her own views. This means that subordinates are more likely to express honest opinions and feelings about the subject in question. Furthermore, it makes it easier for the manager to revise an initial decision, on the basis of the subordinate's comments, without appearing to yield to pressure from the subordinate.

Secondly, the approach can produce higher levels of commitment to the decision on the part of the subordinate. Some subordinates may respond more favourably simply because they appreciate being consulted before the decision is made. Furthermore, the manager can use the Ask phase to gauge how the subordinate feels about the subject, and is therefore in a much better position to select a way of telling and selling the decision which is likely to be acceptable to the subordinate. Finally, the approach may, under certain circumstances, represent a quicker way of reaching a decision with a subordinate. Although time is required to obtain the subordinate's views in the first place, this may be less time consuming than telling the subordinate first, only to discover that the subordinate has information which shows the manager's views to be mistaken or irrelevant to the real problem.

On the negative side, even though the subordinate has been consulted beforehand, he or she may still not like the decision the manager has reached. The same problem could, of course, also occur with any of the variants of the Tell approach which we have already described. The particular problem with the Ask and Tell approach is that the subordinate may reveal his or her preferences quite strongly in the Ask phase, only to find that the manager decides that, on balance, some other solution is more appropriate. Some subordinates may feel more prepared to accept the decision because they have been consulted; others, however, may not. Feeling that their opinion has been ignored, they may be more resentful than if they had never been asked in the first place.

Also, there is the question of the 'ownership' of the decision. Whilst the subordinate may have provided information which helped the manager to make the decision, the manager still made the decision itself and told the subordinate what it was. Even if the subordinate agrees with the decision, there is the possibility that he or she might be more committed to it if involved in actually making the decision rather than simply providing information which helped the manager to make it.

The Problem Solving Approach

The Problem Solving approach is quite different from any previously discussed. The manager does not tell the subordinate what he or she has decided. Instead they work as a team in order to identify the solution to a common problem. Ideally, status differences should be minimized so that each can provide information, suggest solutions, evaluate the other's contribution, propose alternative ways of tackling the problem, build on the other's ideas, and so on. A wide variety of verbal components are appropriate when using this approach. Any of the information-gathering components can be used to encourage the subordinate to contribute information, ideas, potential solutions, and so on. Behavioural influence components such as advice, suggestions, promises, praise and explanations are also relevant, although orders, threats, criticism and leading questions should be avoided as these will tend to have an inhibiting effect. Techniques for handling emotion such as apologies and reflectives may be required when tackling sensitive problems, in order to defuse any adverse emotional reactions which might otherwise render rational problem solving impossible. Finally, the gambit 'causal analysis' can provide a useful way of analyzing sensitive performance problems without arousing adverse emotional reactions.

Used in appropriate circumstances, the Problem Solving approach can have considerable benefits. It encourages the generation of new ideas and the discovery of novel solutions to problems. It is forward looking, and thus avoids the necessity of evaluating the subordinate or the subordinate's past performance and the resentment which can arise when past mistakes are criticized. The whole emphasis is on finding solutions to problems, and it is therefore likely to lead to clear-cut conclusions concerning the ways in which the problem can be avoided in future. This in itself is likely to be motivational as far as the subordinate is concerned, and the fact that the solution is at least in part the subordinate's own may further increase his or her commitment to it. Finally, use of the Problem Solving approach gives the subordinate the opportunity to practise his or her problem solving skills and receive feedback and guidance from the manager, which can enhance the development of these skills.

Inevitably, however, there are also situations in which this approach may be inappropriate. If the subordinate is inexperienced then he or she may not have any ideas concerning the ways in which the problem can be solved. Indeed, if participation in problem solving is invited in a way which suggests that the new subordinate *should* have sufficient knowledge to contribute ideas, this could even arouse anxiety. As we have already noted some employees prefer to be told rather than invited to participate. They may take the view that the manager receives extra pay and status for making decisions, so why should the manager expect them to do his or her job as well? Alternatively the manager may know from past experience that when invited to participate in problem solving, the subordinate typically comes up with impractical or organizationally unacceptable ideas and becomes resentful and uncooperative when these are not accepted. Thus, as the subordinate may have to be told eventually, it would be better to start with a Tell, rather than raise false expectations that his or her views are likely to influence the decision. Finally, the Problem Solving approach is inappropriate when the manager has little room for manoeuvre with respect to the decision to be made. The manager may be constrained by orders, or have come to the conclusion that only one solution is possible on the basis of his or her own analysis of the situation. It would be counterproductive to use the Problem Solving approach to give an illusion of participation, but nevertheless arrive at the manager's decision by pointing out flaws in each of the subordinate's suggestions. The subordinate is almost certain to realize what is happening and become extremely resentful of both the dishonesty and the waste of his or her time.

The Ask and Listen Approach

Using the Ask and Listen approach, the manager asks the subordinate about some problem area and listens to the replies without advancing opinions of his or her own. This can be an appropriate technique in two main situations. Firstly, it can be used to gather information which may help the manager to make a later decision. For example, the manager may wish to obtain the subordinate's views about a possible transfer some time in the future or obtain data and opinions about equipment performance in order to plan future purchasing policy. In other words, the decision cannot be made immediately, involves other people within the organization, or is an inappropriate one for someone at the subordinate's level. Thus the best the manager can do is to assure the subordinate that his or her views will be taken into account and, where appropriate, that he or she will be informed of the decision as soon as possible. When using the Ask and Listen approach for this purpose, all the information gathering components would be relevant, as would the 'funnel technique'.

The other main use of this approach is to give the subordinate the opportunity to talk about a problem which is causing him or her concern. As we have already noted, there is little point in trying to get someone who is emotional to solve a problem rationally. In addition, suggesting solutions before obtaining all the facts is likely to be ineffective, as the subordinate may then produce additional information which invalidates the solution. If the manager genuinely wishes to help, therefore, it is better to encourage the subordinate to talk about the problem without suggesting solutions until the subordinate has calmed down and/or explained the situation in detail. This is an extremely difficult technique. It involves asking questions, listening carefully to the answers, and refusing to be drawn into premature attempts to provide answers to the problem. Thus the main emphasis is upon information-gathering components, particularly those which will encourage the subordinate to talk at length. Inhibitors should be avoided, as should probes if the subordinate is discussing some sensitive area which could cause resentment or embarrassment. Apologies and reflectives may also be useful techniques for reducing adverse emotional reactions should these occur. Ultimately, it may emerge that the problem is simply not solvable. However, the manager has at least given the subordinate the opportunity to talk about it and this is often comforting in itself. If, on the other hand, it appears that the problem is solvable, then the manager can switch to one of the other approaches in an attempt to achieve a solution.

The Ask and Listen approach is, of course, inappropriate when there is a work problem to resolve which requires action on the part of the subordinate. Collecting information may be a necessary first step towards the solution of the problem, but to ensure that the problem is solved rather than merely discussed, a clearly defined plan of action must be drawn up and the subordinate's commitment to it obtained. For this purpose, the Problem Solving approach or one of the Tell approaches would be more appropriate.

The various approaches we have discussed in this section are summarized in Table 6.

CONSIDERATION

The approaches discussed in the previous section differ mainly with respect to the amount of influence which the manager is prepared to allow the subordinate to have over the content of an interaction and its outcome. As we noted earlier, however, there is another way in which managers' approaches to interactions can vary. This is in the extent to which they show consideration for the subordinate's feelings and needs. Thus it would be possible to carry out each of the six approaches in a warm, friendly and concerned manner or in a harsh, cold and uncaring fashion. Note that we are not here concerned with the feelings of the manager, but with the extent to which consideration is shown and its effect on the interaction.

Both verbal and nonverbal cues are relevant here. As we have indicated there is a range of questions and statements which can be used in any one type of interaction. In each case, however, it is possible to select alternative questions and statements which show greater or less consideration. For example, when using one of the various Tell approaches, it is possible to employ orders backed up with threats or to employ advice or requests supported by explanations. It may be that in reality the subordinate has no more freedom to disregard the advice or request than the order, but the effect on the subordinate's feeling and future behaviour could be quite different. Similarly, information gathering in the Tell and Listen, Ask and Tell, and Ask and Listen approaches can be carried out using open questions, and others which encourage the subordinate to talk freely, or using probes, closed and leading questions, which could turn the interaction into an interrogation rather than a discussion.

Even more important are the nonverbal cues. As we showed in Chapter 5, it is possible to show greater friendliness and minimize differences in status and power by such things as smiling, talking more softly, standing or sitting closer to the subordinate, sitting at the same side of the table or across the corner, not interrupting, looking towards the subordinate more when he or she speaks, looking less when one speaks oneself and so on. Conversely, looking stern, talking loudly, interrupting, standing or sitting at a greater distance, sitting on opposite sides of the table, staring at subordinates whilst one is speaking oneself, looking away more when the subordinate is speaking, and so on, will emphasize differences in status and show less friendliness towards the subordinate.

We also pointed out in Chapter 5, that verbal and nonverbal messages need not be consistent with each other. Thus the nonverbal cues which accompany an order could soften its impact making it appear more like a request. Conversely, other nonverbal cues accompanying a request could signal that the

TABLE 6 Approaches to Manager–Subordinate Interactions

Approach	Description	Potential Advantages	Potential Disadvantages	Typical Components
Tell	The manager tells the subordinate the decision, without asking his/her opinions or giving any specific inducements to accept it	Saves time, particularly in emergencies. May be useful as a last resort, when other methods fail	Useful information may be ignored. Subordinates may resent the approach and be reluctant to comply	Orders, requests, suggestions, advice
Tell and Sell	The manager tells the subordinate the decision pointing out the advantages of compliance and/or disadvantages of non-compliance	Can be brief and to the point, getting the message over in a clear, precise and unequivocal manner	Inhibition of independent judgement, defensiveness, overt conflict or passive acceptance without motivation to change	Orders, explanations, requests, praise, threats, promises, leading, inhibitors, criticism, summaries
Tell and Listen	The manager tells the subordinate the decision then allows expression of his/her thoughts or feelings about it	Decreased defensiveness more favourable attitude towards the manager, less resistance to change may result	Can develop into cosy chat with no clear cut conclusions. Overt conflict or passive acceptance may still occur	Orders, requests, praise, criticism, **then** open, comparisons hypotheticals, lubricators
Ask and Tell	The manager asks the subordinate for his/her views on a problem before telling him/her the decision	Solution is less likely to be irrelevant. The subordinate may be more motivated having been consulted	Subordinate may still feel his/her solution to be better and resent being told what to do	Open, probes, comparisons, hypotheticals, lubricators, closed, restatements, summary, **then** orders, requests, leading, threats, promises
Problem Solving	The manager and subordinate analyze a problem together and attempt to find a mutually acceptable solution	Generation of new ideas, development of clear-cut solutions, subordinate highly motivated	Subordinate may lack ideas, produce impractical or organizationally unacceptable solutions, or be unwilling to participate	Open, probes, comparisons, hypotheticals, lubricators, bridges, restatements, summaries, praise, advice, explanation, reflectives
Ask and Listen	The manager asks the subordinate to talk about some problem area and listens attentively	Subordinate may feel much better having discussed the problem. Useful information may be gained	The basic problem may remain unresolved	Open, comparisons, hypotheticals, lubricators, reflectives

subordinate is expected to comply without question. Nevertheless, the combination of verbal and nonverbal cues can make a marked difference to the manner in which a manager conducts an interaction with a subordinate even though the amount of participation allowed in decision making might be the same in both cases.

Again, which approach is most appropriate will depend on the circumstances. Two main factors are involved—the likely response of the subordinate and the extent to which compliance is essential. Consideration tends to produce more satisfied subordinates.[2] Thus, if the subordinate will supply the information required or comply with the manager's wishes when asked in a considerate manner, there seems little point in risking the negative consequences which can result from having dissatisfied subordinates by using a less considerate approach. The danger of using a considerate approach, however, is that the subordinate may feel that the manager is not serious in expecting compliance or will not react too unfavourably if the subordinate decides not to conform to the manager's wishes. For example, Burns[3] found that tactfully-given instructions from superiors were interpreted as information or advice, and Argyle[4] points out that, for all its advantages, the persuasive/democratic style can be very misleading to those who are not used to it. A less considerate approach is therefore appropriate when both the following conditions apply. Firstly, compliance on the part of the subordinate is essential, either because there is an emergency and there is no time for niceties, or because the manager has thought the problem through and come to the conclusion that there would be serious repercussions if the subordinate does not respond in a certain way. Secondly, past experience has shown that the subordinate does not respond when treated with consideration, and will only comply with the manager's wishes when the latter 'lays it on the line' in a businesslike manner.

CHANGING APPROACH DURING AN INTERACTION

So far, we have assumed for the sake of convenience that the manager will use the same approach throughout an interaction with a subordinate. However, this need not necessarily be the case. Sometimes a change in approach may be appropriate because the subordinate does not respond as expected. Suppose, for example, the subordinate responds to a Tell and Sell approach by indicating that he or she does not accept the managers interpretation of the situation. The manager may then Tell and Sell more vigorously, which can have adverse consequences in some circumstances (see 'Win—lose syndrome' later in the chapter). Alternatively, the manager may decide to try a different approach, e.g. Ask and Listen or Problem Solving, in order to accommodate the subordinate's views. Managers may also change approach during an interaction because they feel that different approaches provide more appropriate ways of handling differing topics during an interaction. For example, they may Tell where compliance is essential (e.g. conforming with safety regulations) Ask and Listen with respect to the subordinate's domestic problems and Problem Solve with respect to a problem of mutual interest (e.g. coping with effects of late deliveries).

To be able to change approaches in this way requires a higher level of interpersonal skills than the mere mastery of each approach in isolation. In particular, it requires the sophisticated use of bridges, not only between topics, but also between approaches and the manner in which the interaction is conducted. If handled badly, such a transition could affect the interaction adversely. The subordinate may resent being asked at one moment, only to be told the next, because his or her responses were not what the manager wanted to hear. However, managers with greater interpersonal skills are likely to be more flexible, and have the ability to use a variety of different approaches within the same interaction, moving smoothly from one to the other.

SYNDROMES

The approaches which we have described represent the manager's intentions with respect to an interaction. Inevitably, however, things do not always work out as intended. For example, the manager may intend to Tell and Sell, but the subordinate may not listen to what the manager has to say and refuse to 'buy' any of the manager's solutions. Faced with this kind of situation, the interpersonally skilled manager will be able to adapt his or her approach and/or the related verbal and nonverbal components, and thus still carry out a successful interaction. A less skilful manager, on the other hand, may find that an approach is not working, but fail to find a way of remedying the situation, resulting in an interaction which conspicuously fails to meet his or her objectives.

In our experience, approaches which 'go wrong' often do so in similar ways. Thus, it is possible to identify certain types of interaction which occur when the approach selected by the manager fails to work as intended. We have called these failed interactions syndromes, their symptoms being the cluster of components and structural devices typically associated with them. Some of the syndromes which we have encountered in the course of interpersonal skills training are given below. In each case, we have described what we believe to be the underlying cause of the syndrome, its major symptoms, and actions which can be taken to rectify the situation.

1. The Preconceived Ideas Syndrome

Underlying Cause
The manager has already decided what the facts of the case and the required solution(s) are before an interaction with a subordinate begins.

Major Symptoms

- Leading questions (to gain compliance with preconceived ideas)
- Closed questions (to tidy up any minor points of detail)
- Inhibitors (to prevent the subordinate from talking at length on 'irrelevant' matters)
- Not listening
- Interrupting
- Talking much more than the subordinate

Remedial Action

Syndrome level. Treating information as hypothesis rather than fact.
Symptom level
- More open questions (to get subordinate talking)
- More lubricators (to keep subordinate talking)
- More restatements (to check understanding of points raised by the subordinate)
- Active listening (particularly listening and watching for nonverbal cues of agreement, disagreement, surprise, frustration, etc. as well as the verbal content)

2. The Recycling Syndrome

Underlying Causes

The manager has not thought through the ramifications of the problem areas before the discussion and feels that he/she needs more time to think, or is unwilling to face up to the emotional conflict which might arise if problem areas are probed too deeply.

Major Symptoms

- The manager moves on to another topic before coming to an agreed conclusion concerning the topic under discussion
- The manager periodically returns to the same topic or topics, interspersed with discussions of other subjects
- The subordinate may reintroduce topics left unfinalized by the manager either (a) there is no summary of agreed future actions (because none exist) or (b) when the manager attempts to summarize, the subordinate objects that he/she never agreed to these actions

Remedial Action

Syndrome level
- Thinking through likely problem areas before the discussion
- Being more prepared to face up to emotional conflict (a largely useless piece of advice unless backed up with training on *how* to do it at the technique level)

- Delaying closure on a topic until a full agreed solution is arrived at

Symptom level
- More probes (to obtain detailed information about the problem area under discussion)
- More restatements (to ensure that the manager is sure he/she understands the subordinate's point of view)
- More tolerance of silence on part of manager (to allow the subordinate some thinking time or force the latter to talk)
- More time spent on defining what the problem is
- Greater participation by the subordinate in problem definition and solution
- Use of causal analysis (as means of avoiding defensive reactions on part of subordinate)
- Practice in use of reflectives (to increase confidence in ability to handle emotional reactions should they arise)

3. The Shopping List Syndrome

Underlying Causes
The manager has decided that there are a number of key points to be covered and arranges them in an apparently logical order. These points are then worked through in a mechanical fashion. Underlying this may be a lack of faith in his/her own skills, or a desire to cover too much ground in the time available, leading to a desire to have everything cut and dried beforehand.

Major Symptoms
- The interaction moves at a relatively high speed covering a lot of points, none in any great depth
- Multiples
- Inhibitors   } To prevent the subordinate deviating from the
- Interruptions   } pre-arranged order
- Closed questions
- Not listening
- Premature closure on superficial solutions
- Signs of frustration and/or non-acceptance on the part of the subordinate

Remedial Action
Syndrome level. Treating plans as agendas, which are useful as guides or checklists, but which need not be rigidly adhered to.

Symptom level
- Asking the subordinate to suggest items for the agenda (e.g. "Here is what I would like to talk about . . . Is there anything else you think we should discuss in this meeting?")
- More open questions (to elicit the subordinate's views)
- Lubricators (to keep him/her talking)
- Active listening

- Closure delaying techniques (e.g. "Before we move on, is there anything else you think we should discuss on this subject?")
- Interim summaries with checks at end of each section (e.g. "What we seem to have agreed so far is that . . . Would you agree?")

4. The Win–Lose Syndrome

Underlying Causes
(a) The manager views interactions with subordinates as a contest which he or she is determined to win and encounters a subordinate who is unwilling to back down.
(b) The manager wishes to have a constructive interaction in which he/she helps the subordinate to improve his performance, and believes that the first step is to get the subordinate to recognize and admit to his/her current failings. The subordinate refuses to do so, and the manager is afraid of loosing face if he/she backs down, or gets annoyed with the 'uncooperative' subordinate, and an argument develops.

Major Symptoms
- Emotional reactions on the part of both manager and subordinate
- Neither is willing to accept the validity of the other's statements
- A large number of critical statements
- Little praise, and what there is is general and qualified (e.g. "Overall, you have done quite well, but . . .")
- Closed questions and leading statements (e.g. "You must realize that . . .")
- Interruptions
- Inhibitors
- Little use of requests, explanations and promises and if used at all, rapidly decline when not 'bought' by the subordinate
- A large number of orders and threats
- Trap setting

Remedial Action
Syndrome level. Look for solutions which are win–win, i.e. will benefit both the manager and subordinate.
Symptom level

- More open questions, comparisons, hypotheticals, lubricators, restatements, etc. (to gain an understanding of the subordinate's viewpoint)
- Active listening (as above)
- Greater use of detailed praise, explanations, requests, advice, etc.
- Replace criticism with causal analysis as a means of introducing the subject of performance improvement

- Use of reflectives, apologies as a means of handling emotional reactions if they do arise.

5. Cosy Chat Syndrome

Underlying Causes
The manager (a) does not believe the problem is sufficiently serious to merit much attention and is merely paying lip-service to it, or (b) feels he or she lacks skills to handle the interaction effectively, and probably fears an adverse reaction from the subordinate should he/she attempt to do so, or (c) wants to maintain an image of being a nice person.

Major Symptoms
- Open questions with no follow through (e.g. "How are things going in general?" . . . "Everything alright?" . . . "Good!")
- General praise
- Vague promises
- Rapid switch to more 'comfortable' topics, such as the weather, sport or office politics

Remedial Action
Syndrome level
- If the problem is genuinely not serious, none
- If it is serious, attempt to influence the motivation of the manager (e.g. by carrying out a behavioural influence interview with the manager *or*
- Provide interpersonal skills training for the manager

Symptom level. Greater precision in use of all components.

6. The Good Information Gatherer

Underlying Cause
The manager has excellent information gathering skills, but once having gathered the information does nothing with it.

Major Symptoms
- Skilful use of a wide variety of information gathering components ("Tell me about it")
- Manager does not initiate any discussion of future actions to improve performance of the subordinate
- Manager does not take up any attempts by subordinate to discuss ways of improving performance.

Remedial Action
Syndrome level. Re-examination of objectives of discussion, to draw out the

importance of emphasis on behavioural influence.

Symptom level

- Identification of possible areas of performance improvement and ways to achieve it, before the interaction
- Use of information-gathering skills to identify areas where the subordinate feels he/she could improve his/her performance (e.g. "What do you think you might have done differently?")
- Where the subordinate cannot solve his/her own problems, the use of behavioural influence components to persuade the subordinate to change his or her behaviour in the desired direction.
- Use of restatements and summaries to ensure agreement concerning performance problems and future courses of action.

7. The Bought 'Easy Ride' Syndrome

Underlying Cause
The manager wishes to have as painless an interaction as possible, and therefore identifies what the subordinate wants and gives it to him/her unconditionally.

Major Symptoms

- A large amount of recognition and general praise
- Promises given as a 'gift'
- No discussion of performance improvement

Remedial Action
Syndrome level. A recognition that increasing job satisfaction will not necessarily improve performance.

Symptom level

- Use of information gathering skills to identify and agree areas where performance improvement could be achieved, and specific ways to achieve it
- Where necessary, use of behavioural influence skills to obtain commitment to the ways of achieving performance improvement

The main use which we would envisage for these syndromes is in interpersonal skills training. Often, advice on how to improve interpersonal skills can be given in terms of components, the way the interaction is structured or the approach taken. For example, supposing a tutor wishes to give feedback to a leadership trainee who has just carried out a practice interaction which did not achieve its objectives. The interviewee asked many closed and leading questions, interrupted a great deal, did not listen to what the 'subordinate' had to say, and thus missed important information, resulting in mistaken or irrelevant conclusions being drawn. The tutor feels that the interaction could have been more productive had the manager used more open questions and probes, listened more closely to the subordinate, let the subordinate finish what he or she had to say, and taken the subordinates views into account in deciding future courses of action. Such advice would be much easier to remember if organized in some meaningful way, and the components used in an interaction, even a failed one, are often related to some common underlying cause. In this case, the trainee may have behaved as described because of a mistaken belief that he or she already knew the facts of the case and what should be done to solve the problem, and therefore did not need to obtain any further information from the subordinate.

Thus, the task of improving interpersonal skills can be tackled not only in terms of verbal and nonverbal components, but also as a syndrome (Preconceived Ideas). This has a number of advantages. Firstly, it provides a unifying explanatory concept which will enable the trainee to remember and recognize the various undesirable symptoms more readily. Secondly, if the trainee understands the underlying problem, then this may assist the achievement of a solution. For example, the concept of treating data as hypotheses rather than established facts provides a rationale for the substitution of information gathering components for those previously used. Not only will this help the manager to remember them, but he or she may also be led by this strategy to use other appropriate information gathering components or gambits, in addition to those specifically mentioned by the tutor. Finally, and most importantly, understanding why the previous behaviour was inappropriate in a certain set of circumstances, and why another approach would be more successful, will enable the manager to be more skilful in selecting the right approach in future. Simply telling a trainee to stop using leading and closed questions and use more open questions and lubricators is not very good advice because he or she will undoubtedly encounter situation's where closed and leading questions are appropriate, and open questions and lubricators are inappropriate.

CONCLUSIONS

In this chapter we have looked at various ways of describing a manager's overall approach to an interaction with a subordinate. We have suggested that this can vary with respect to the amount of influence which the manager is prepared to allow the subordinate, and the consideration which the manager shows towards the subordinate during the interaction. Finally, we described some typical examples of unsuccessful interactions, and suggested ways in which they can be avoided or the situation rectified if they do occur.

We realize that by including approaches in our model of the interpersonal skills of leadership, we are close to reintroducing the concept of leadership style which we criticized earlier. However, there is an important difference. As we have already pointed out, leadership style theorists describe leadership behaviour only in very general terms and do not identify the specific behaviours associated with any one style. The approaches described in this chapter, on the other hand, are closely associated with the use of certain verbal and nonverbal components and structural devices. Thus the approaches are, in a sense, convenient shorthand for commonly occurring clusters of such components and structural devices.

Furthermore, our approach emphasizes leadership as a skill, considering not only what leaders do, but how well they do it. As we noted in Chapter 1, we would regard the interpersonally skilled leader as one who:

- has a wide variety of verbal components (question and statement types) at his or her disposal and is able to select the one most appropriate for the situation and particular purpose at hand, and perform it well, with the appropriate nonverbal cues;
- is able to structure interactions effectively by linking these components into purposeful sequences which impel the interaction towards its objective(s);
- is able to develop an approach to the interaction, which is appropriate to the objectives in question and the probable reactions of the subordinate.

In leadership training, the interactions between these levels are of particular importance. It is of little use attempting to change a manager's overall approach unless the component skills are also taught or in some way developed. It is all very well persuading an authoritarian manager that a Tell and Sell approach is not always appropriate and that he or she should use a more participative Problem Solving approach under certain circumstances. However, unless the manager knows and can use effectively the components of a participative approach—open questions, reflectives, etc.—he or she is unlikely to make a *good* participative manager. One may simply exchange an inappropriate style done well for an appropriate style poorly done, and it is anyone's guess which would be the more ineffective. Equally, however, attempting to improve leadership skills in terms of components alone also has its limitations. Without higher-level unifying concepts, trainees are reduced to learning an apparently random list of techniques, which is likely both to make the task more difficult and to reduce the motivation to learn. Concentration at any level of analysis, to the exclusion of others, is therefore likely to impair the effectiveness of leadership skills training.

In the next chapter we will examine the acquisition and development of leadership skills in more detail.

REFERENCES

1   NRF Maier (1958), 'Three Types of Appraisal Interview', *Personnel*, Vol. 34, pp. 27–40.

2   RM Stogdill (1974), *Handbook of Leadership*, Free Press.

3   T Burns (1954), 'The Directions of Activity and Communication in a Departmental Executive Group: A Quantitative Study in a British Engineering Factory with a Self-recording Technique', *Human Relations*, Vol. 7, pp. 73–97.

4   M Argyle (1975), *Bodily Communication*, Methuen.

Chapter 8

The Acquisition and Development of Leadership Skills

INTRODUCTION

Previous chapters have been concerned with developing an understanding of the interpersonal skills of leadership. In this chapter we shall concentrate upon the development of the skills themselves. Like other complex skills, interpersonal skills require *practice* to achieve a high level of performance.

However, practice is not in itself sufficient to produce an improvement in skilled performance. Feedback is also necessary. Without feedback the trainee cannot assess whether any further improvement in performance is desirable, and if so, what forms it should take. There are two main forms of feedback, intrinsic and extrinsic. Intrinsic feedback arises directly from the task itself, e.g. asking a question and listening to the kind of response one receives. Extrinsic feedback, on the other hand, comes from some external source, such as a tutor, one's boss or colleagues. Extrinsic feedback is particularly important in the early stages of skills development, when the trainee may not be sure which aspects of performance he or she should be attending to, but intrinsic feedback becomes more important as the skill develops.[1]

Formal training courses, designed to provide practice with feedback and guidance from skilled tutors, represent one of the most effective ways of acquiring interpersonal skills, particularly in the early stages of skills development. In this chapter, though, we shall be concerned as much with the *self* development of leadership skills as with their acquisition through formal training. To provide a framework for our discussion we shall first describe a model of manager–subordinate interactions, which identifies the key interpersonal variables involved and the relationships between them.

A MODEL OF MANAGER–SUBORDINATE INTERACTIONS

Figure 6 presents a model, setting out what we consider to be the interpersonal variables which strongly influence manager–subordinate interactions. It is intended to help both individual managers, and tutors on formal training courses, to analyze the processes involved in manager–subordinate interactions and to identify the specific aspects of the manager's behaviour which are tending to produce less satisfactory outcomes.

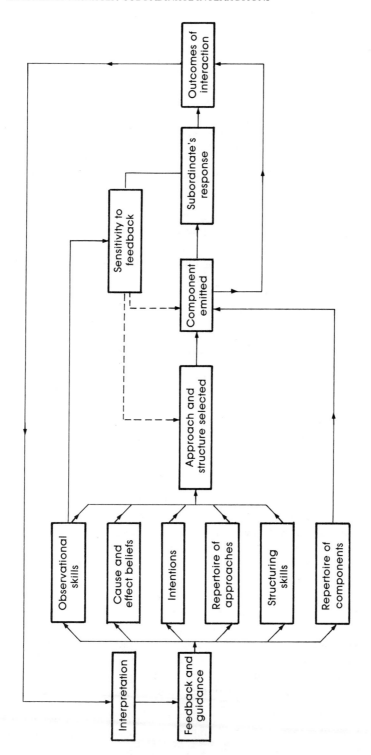

FIGURE 6 Interaction and Tutoring Processes in Manager–Subordinate Interactions

The model suggests that the behaviour of a manager in an interaction with a subordinate can be described in terms of:

(a) The manager's general approach to the interaction, e.g. Ask and Listen, Tell and Sell, etc.
(b) The way in which the manager structures the interaction, i.e. diffuse or organized
(c) The actual verbal and nonverbal components used with such an approach/ structure, e.g. open questions, probes, orders.

The actual approach, structure and components selected by the manager will depend on a number of factors. The range of options open to the manager will be determined by his or her:

(a) Repertoire of approaches—the number of different approaches the manager is capable of utilizing well
(b) Structuring skills—the ability to develop an effective interaction structure, either before or during the interaction
(c) Repertoire of components—the number of different components the manager is capable of utilizing well.

Within the range of options available, the choice of approach, structure and components is likely further to be influenced by the manager's:

(d) Intentions—what the manager wishes to achieve from the interaction, e.g. gather information, solve a performance problem, listen to a grievance, deliver a reprimand.
(e) Cause and effect beliefs—the manager's expectations that using a particular approach, structure or type of component will lead the subordinate to respond in a certain way, thus producing certain outcomes, desirable or undesirable. An example of such a belief might be: "If I tell subordinates exactly what is expected of them, and point out the rewards and punishment involved, they will know where they stand, and do as they are told." Such beliefs may be conscious or unconscious, and clearly or vaguely articulated. One overriding belief which will influence the way the manager conducts the interaction is whether he or she believes there is only one correct way to conduct manager–subordinate interactions. Obviously, a manager who believes this is likely to have a narrow repertoire of approaches, structures and components.
(f) Observational skills—the manager's ability to interpret the subordinate's manner at the beginning of the interaction, particularly nonverbal signals of mood indicating whether he or she is enthusiastic, depressed, angry, apathetic and so on. Depending on the manager's cause and effect beliefs, such signals, if picked up, may lead the manager to depart from the planned or usual way of conducting the interaction.

Having selected a particular approach, structure and component to initiate the interaction, the manager uses the component, and the subordinate then responds. This response provides a major part of the intrinsic feedback (that arising directly from the task itself). In addition, feedback is also available to the manager concerning his or her own behaviour, e.g. the manager's own tone of voice, phrasing of questions, manner, etc. as it appears to him or herself. The extent to which such feedback is actually registered will be dependent on his or her observational skills—the ability to recognize such things as signs of acceptance or rejection on the part of the subordinate or the vaguely phrased question on the part of the manager. Another factor will be the manager's skill in using different approaches, structures and components. The more skilled the manager, the more he or she will be able to select and perform them without conscious thought, and the more attention this will leave available for observing intrinsic feedback.

If relevant intrinsic feedback is registered by the manager, this may lead him or her to modify the approach, interaction structure, or type of component used. On the other hand, less sensitive managers, or those who are insufficiently flexible to change their approach mid-interaction, may ignore quite obvious feedback (hence the dotted lines in Figure 6). Other sources of inflexibility are the manager's cause and effect beliefs and skill in handling different approaches. Thus the manager may register the subordinate's adverse responses, but ignore them because he or she believes that the approach taken is the only effective way to treat subordinates, or does not know how to handle the situation differently.

Finally, by the end of the interaction, certain outcomes will have resulted. Three types of outcome may be distinguished and may occur either singly or in combination:

- Motivational/emotional. The subordinate—and manager—may feel enthusiastic or apathetic, satisfied or dissatisfied, and so on with respect to the conduct of the interaction or what it achieved.
- Informational. Did the manager and subordinate obtain from each other in a precise form any information which they may have required?
- Behavioural. Did the manager agree on a precise set of actions—to be carried out either by manager or subordinate or both—to rectify any performance problem which has been identified?

FORMAL TRAINING COURSES IN THE INTERPERSONAL SKILLS OF LEADERSHIP

As we noted earlier, formal training courses which provide an opportunity to practise with feedback and guidance from skilled tutors, represent one of the most effective ways of developing interpersonal skills. They have two main advantages. Firstly, they allow the trainee to practise the skills in a relatively risk-free, supportive environment, away from the manager's daily routine. Typically, such courses use role playing exercises which allow the individual to practise a skill in a situation which approximates to real life, and receive feedback on his or her performance, without the disruptive effect this might have on real life relationships. Furthermore, research which has been carried into interpersonal skills training using role playing shows that new skills are acquired which do transfer to the workplace.[2] A more detailed description of a typical course using the 'Bradford Approach' to interpersonal skills training is given in Appendix IV. The second major advantage of formal training courses is that they allow the manager to obtain feedback and guidance from a skilled tutor. Such feedback and guidance is likely to be of a higher quality and more pertinent than that obtained through self analysis or from fellow managers or other untrained observers. The result is that early learning is likely to take place at a more rapid pace. People who are relatively unskilled, either at the activity in question or in giving feedback, can still provide helpful feedback. Nevertheless, they are unlikely to be able to pinpoint quite so accurately as a skilled tutor, the precise learning point which the manager most needs to work on next.

A number of factors are involved here. Firstly, there is the question of selectivity. Of all the things which happened in the course of the interaction, which had most effect on what was, or was not achieved? Similarly, of all the things which the trainee *could* improve, which should be worked on *next*? Secondly, there is the question of interpretation. A recorded playback of an interaction may reveal *what* happened but not *why*. Suppose a manager uses a moderately forceful Tell and Sell approach and merely achieves the reluctant compliance of the subordinate. The manager may assume that this was because he or she did not put his or her ideas forcefully enough and was too lenient. An alternative, and perhaps more valid, interpretation might be that the manager expressed his or her ideas *too* forcefully, and the subordinate might have been more committed had he or she been allowed to contribute more to the discussion. Finally, there is the question of the action(s) to be taken to improve performance in similar situations in future. Again, differing views are possible. The manager in the previous example may feel that he or she should be less soft in future and immediately stamp on any attempt by the subordinate to take control of the interaction. An alternative view might be that, under certain circumstances, it would be better to allow the subordinate to participate in making decisions rather than simply tell him or her what to do. In other words, the mere availability of feedback does not necessarily mean that a trainee will be able to make good use of it. Indeed, if the trainee draws inappropriate conclusions from the feedback or becomes demoralized because he or she cannot see how to improve an apparently inadequate performance, then detailed feedback may even be counterproductive. It is for this reason that the help of a skilled tutor is invaluable in the early stages of skills acquisition.

We would suggest that the interpersonal skills tutor has two main functions. The first is an immediate function of helping the trainee to decide what should be worked on next to improve performance and what should be done differently in order to achieve this improvement. In part, this will involve giving or eliciting feedback about what happened in the interaction and why, but in moving from this stage to what should be done to improve performance in future, we have moved imperceptibly from feedback to guidance. In our view, this is one of the primary functions of the interpersonal skills tutor. Unless the trainee has a clear idea of what to do next in order to perform better, then he or she is unlikely to improve to any great extent.

The particular aspects of performance selected to work on next will depend not only on their influence on the trainee's performance, but also on the trainee's ability to make significant improvements in these areas at this stage of his or her skill development. It may be better to improve a relatively minor skill than attempt to rectify a major shortcoming and fail. Similarly, the number of improvements attempted needs careful thought. If too many different steps are identified, this may both confuse and demoralize the trainee: two or three things to work on at a time is usually sufficient. The specific points selected for feedback and guidance may relate to any of the processes identified in our model of manager–subordinate interactions. Thus the manager could be given feedback concerning the approach and interaction structure selected, the components used, the way in which the subordinate responded, the extent to which the manager appeared to adapt to these responses, and the outcomes apparently achieved by the end of the interaction. Next, any relationships between these processes could be drawn out. For example, were the subordinate's responses during the interaction the result of the particular approach, structure or components used? Did lack of sensitivity to feedback lead to important information being missed? Did the outcomes achieve the intentions the manager had at the beginning of the interaction? As noted previously, such feedback is likely to be highly selective. Particular aspects of the interaction will be chosen to be discussed, but the tutor needs to be able to understand and monitor all of them in order to make an appropriate choice.

Finally, the tutor may give guidance on how to conduct a more effective interaction should similar circumstances arise again. Such guidance can be classified in terms of the factors listed in Figure 6 which determine the type of interaction the manager chooses to carry out.

- *Observational Skills* Guidance on whether the manager needs to pay more attention to nonverbal cues, which cues to watch out for, what they signify, and so on.
- *Cause and Effect Beliefs* Guidance on which approaches, structures and components are more appropriate for different purposes, people and situations.
- *Intentions* Guidance on whether certain intentions are appropriate in certain circumstances, e.g. the purposes of certain kinds of formal interactions such as grievance or performance appraisal interviews.
- *Repertoire of Approaches*
  (i) Expansion of the repertoire of approaches by giving information about an alternative approach not already in the manager's repertoire.

(ii) Guidance on how to perform an existing approach more skilfully.

- *Structuring Skills* Guidance on how to structure interactions more skilfully by such methods as forward planning, agreeing an agenda within the interaction, using components such as bridges and summaries, and the need for flexibility and so on.
- *Repertoire of Components*
  (i) Expansion of the repertoire of components by describing other components not already within the manager's repertoire.
  (ii) Guidance on how to perform an existing component more skilfully.

The tutor will certainly not wish to give guidance on all these topics, but it is necessary to be aware of all of them in order to decide on which to concentrate.

The second, more long term function of the tutor is to develop the trainee's ability to become his or her own source of feedback, interpretation and guidance, so that the trainee can go on improving his or her skill without the help of a tutor.[3] Even at the early stage of training, the tutor can, in addition to providing the extrinsic feedback so important at this stage, lay the foundations for the later use of intrinsic feedback to continue skill development once the course is over.

Like any other skills, the skills of attending to feedback, interpreting it and planning one's own performance improvement are acquired most easily through practice with feedback and guidance. Thus if these skills are to be acquired during a training session, the tutor must give the trainee the opportunity to practise them, and also provide feedback and guidance on the trainee's performance. The Problem Solving approach described in Chapter 7 is ideal for this purpose. The tutor can ask open questions, such as: "How far do you think you achieved your objectives?", "What was it that you did in the course of the interaction which had the biggest effect on what was achieved?" and "What could you have done differently in order to have achieved more from the interaction?". If necessary, such questions can be followed up by probes, comparisons, hypotheticals to obtain more precise information, and recognition to reinforce insightful comments. The immediate aim is to guide the manager to reach his or her own conclusions, which are both appropriate and explicit enough to be acted upon in the manager's next interaction of a similar type. This guidance may take the form of helping the manager to sharpen up vague conclusions or consider alternatives to less appropriate conclusions by the use of skilful questionning technique. The long term aim is to encourage managers periodically to analyze subsequent interactions in the same way, and give them practice in the skills involved so that they will be able to analyze their own performance in much the same terms as the tutor would if he or she were there. For example:

- How did that interaction go on the whole?
- How far do I think I met my objectives?
- What were the major things that I did which influenced how much I achieved?

- What could I have done differently which could have enabled me to achieve more?

Of course, even tutors sometimes choose the wrong approach. It may happen that the trainee manager either can't or won't come up with suggestions for improving his or her interpersonal skills, or the manager may give what the tutor thinks are highly inappropriate solutions, and there is simply insufficient time to achieve more appropriate conclusions using a Problem Solving approach. In this case, the tutor may be reduced to using the clear and quick Tell and Sell approach. As a last resort, a told solution is probably better than no solution at all, despite depriving the manager of the opportunity to practise and gain feedback and guidance on his or her skills of self development.

On courses using the Bradford Approach to interpersonal skills training, a further opportunity to practise self development skills is provided in the final plenary session of each day (see Appendix IV). One problem with this kind of training, however, is that it is labour intensive. A skilled tutor is necessary in each syndicate group and the groups will necessarily be small to give each member adequate opportunity to practise.

Outside of these training groups, the problem is, in effect, one of finding substitutes for the skilled tutor which would enable the manager to take over the various tasks of selection, feedback, interpretation and guidance described earlier in this chapter. This problem is taken up in the next section.

SELF DEVELOPMENT APPROACHES TO THE ACQUISITION OF INTERPERSONAL SKILLS

The Role of Feedback in Skill Development

It is worth re-emphasizing here that the extent to which feedback is available and registered is dependent upon the manager's knowledge of the important variables which influence an interaction and his or her ability to observe the effects of them on a subordinate in an interaction. This latter will improve as the manager becomes more skilful since one of the aspects of skilled performance is that skilled performers do not need to concentrate on their actions. With this reduction in apparent mental effort comes the additional ability to attend selectively to the processes occurring in the interaction. The skilled motorist simply drives somewhere—he or she doesn't have to concentrate on what the arms or legs are doing. Similarly, the person skilled in the interpersonal skills of leadership doesn't think about questions and statements, and non-verbal cues, but of objectives. Once the objective of the interaction is clear, the questions and statements, and non-verbal cues automatically occur in the required way to suit the objectives. But where to begin?

There seems to be three overlapping phases in the development of interpersonal skills. The first is the Preparation Phase in which learning the basic material occurs. This includes the basic components—the types of questions and their purpose, non-verbal cues and so on—from which interactions are built. This is the book learning phase.

The second phase or Structuring Phase is directly related to the development of structuring skills, that is, how to structure an interaction. It often requires the modification or 'unlearning' of existing conceptual structures relating to interpersonal interactions and the development of new ones. For example, old word habits such as asking leading questions and closed questions to gather information may need to be compared with, and modified to incorporate, the alternative approach of asking open questions and probes in order to achieve certain outcomes. Expansion of the repertoire of approaches and their common components—being able to Tell and Sell or Problem-Solve when required—is another aspect. Unlike the previous phase, this phase needs both practice and feedback. It also requires a lot of effort, and in terms of achieving skilled performance it is the most important phase. The consequent improvement in skill leads to the third phase, the Refinement Phase.

The Refinement Phase is characterized by efficient performance where questions and statements and styles and approaches automatically occur once the objective of the interaction is clear. It involves the application of knowledge and conceptual structures into smooth and efficient performance to suit individual situations. Performance at this level characterizes the expert and usually requires long hours of practice with feedback.

These three phases, then, give a guide to how to develop the skills required for successful performance. Initially the most important learning in the Preparation Phase is that of the question and statement types (the Repertoire of Components in Figure 1) and the Repertoire of Approaches (these are discussed in Chapters 4, 5 and 7 respectively). However, this is not the only learning in this phase, but it is sufficient to provide a basis for phase two: practising, implementing and structuring the skills. In the first instance, when learning the basic question and statement types it is worth trying to formulate examples of them for different circumstances. Hearing yourself formulating and saying these components will help you learn them more quickly and apply them with a more appropriate tone of voice etc. You can even imagine answers which will help you to formulate your next question and so on.

The next stage of practice is testing out your learning in an actual conversation. You can do this immediately within your organization on your subordinates and peers, or, if you wish to check both that you have adequately learned the techniques and they really do achieve what we claim, then you can use them anywhere. In restaurants (''Can you tell me about the dishes?''—open question; ''What are the ingredients of the sauce?''—probe/closed question, etc.), in bars (''What do you think about the local football team?'', ''What difference do you think Jones would make to the team if he replaced Jordan?'', etc.), in the home, and so on. Children are frequently good for practising your techniques on reticent individuals. Asking ''How did your day at school go today?'' is likely to bring one or two words of response of the sort "All right", or "Not bad" or "Same as usual". Where do you go from there? The tendency for people unskilled in this area is to immediately start asking closed or leading questions of the sort "Did you have history?" or "You did some English and maths didn't you?". This limits the information gathering and probably stops the conversation fairly rapidly. Instead one could probe the answer "What do you mean by all right?", or try another open—"Tell me about it". Trying to keep a conversation going with children can be extremely difficult and is thus excellent practice.

As you practise these conversations, other factors relevant to the overall activity become apparent, for example, nonverbal cues (see Chapter 5). Are you paying enough attention to them? Which cues should you watch out for in each situation? What do they signify? These are phase one learning variables, but they cannot be observed and learned without second phase activity. This is why the phases are described as overlapping.

Once you have implemented some form of practice, you need to consciously use the techniques and extend their use to as many appropriate situations as possible. In this way your structures, techniques, strategies and tactics will become more naturally suited to your intentions and purposes in the situation. As noted earlier this may prove difficult at first due to the need to 'unlearn' various word habits, beliefs about people and behaviour and approaches to people which have gradually developed over many years. It takes a lot of effort and time, but will eventually be rewarded by achievement of that stage in development where questions, statements, nonverbal behaviour, approaches and structure automatically flow in response to the objectives of the situation.

To help you in this process a self development checklist is presented in Appendix V. In the next section, we describe the checklist and provide guidelines concerning the way it is intended to be used.

The Self Development Checklist

The checklist is intended to be completed shortly after an interaction with a subordinate, in order to help the manager to identify what he or she should be doing differently to carry out such interactions more skilfully. It may be used periodically as a check on how your interpersonal skills are developing or as a means of analyzing a particular interaction which produced less satisfactory outcomes than you would have wished.

Question 1 asks *what were the objectives of the interaction*. In the case of planned interactions, these will be the intentions which you had at the beginning of the interaction. In the case of spontaneous interactions these may be either what you were trying to achieve in the interaction or what you now realize you should have been trying to achieve in the interaction, if these are different.

Question 2 asks *what were the outcomes of the interactions*. Obviously, comparison of the first two questions will give an indication of *how successful the interaction was* (Question 3). Question 4 is concerned with *how a successful interaction could be made even better.* Question 5 seeks to identify *the ways in which the outcomes of an unsuccessful interaction were unsatisfactory.* Question 6 asks *in what ways the manager's handling of the interaction contributed to the unsatisfactory outcomes.* To help managers who may be unsure why a particular interaction was unsuccessful, a number of hypotheses concerning the reasons why interactions may fail are suggested in Appendix VI. We are not saying that all these hypotheses will be relevant or that there might not be other reasons for the problem encountered. Interpersonal relations are far too complex to be able to give hard and fast rules, particularly when the exact circumstances are not known. Rather, the hypotheses are extended as suggestions which might help you to consider a wider variety of options in deciding how to improve your interpersonal skills. If none of our suggestions are relevant then perhaps in thinking why our suggestions do not apply, this will trigger you to think of more relevant ones.

Finally Question 7 asks *what changes you could make in order to carry out a more successful interaction if faced with a similar situation in future.* It asks what your main objective(s) should be. These may be general objectives for this type of interaction, e.g. "Make sure of my facts before criticizing subordinates", or "Ensure that all actions are agreed and summarized before moving on to the next topic". Alternatively, the form can be used to plan for a specific interaction, in which case you may wish to specify exactly what you wish to achieve, e.g. "Find out how Bob would feel about a transfer to another location should one arise" or "Find a way of ensuring that shortage of spare parts does not cause production bottlenecks".

Question 7 also asks *in what ways you would like to carry out the interaction differently in order to obtain more satisfactory outcomes.* Again, this can relate to this type of interaction generally or to a specific interaction with a particular subordinate in the near future. If the latter, then it is of course possible to analyze this later interaction using the checklist to assess how successful you were in achieving your objectives and whether any further improvement is called for. In terms of our model of the processes involved in manager–subordinate interactions (Figure 6), the checklist covers a variety of factors. These include the approach, structure and components used, the subordinate's response and the outcomes of the interaction. Much depends upon the manager's awareness of feedback. A checklist can only ask the manager to think about his or her behaviour and the way the subordinate responds. If, however, the manager thinks he is asking open questions when in fact he is using leading or closed questions or thinks that she has gained commitment when the subordinate has signalled reluctant compliance at most, then there is no way in which a checklist can tell the manager that he or she is wrong. A tempting solution to this problem might be for the manager to solicit feedback from his or her own subordinates after a real life interaction. However, the manager who could most afford to do this is the one with considerable interpersonal skills, and who, therefore, probably is in least need of the feedback. The manager in most need of the feedback is the one with poor interpersonal skills, but this probably means that he or she will solicit the feedback in an unskilled way and will not know how to handle it when he or she receives it. There is a serious danger, therefore, that the manager with relatively poor interpersonal skills, by soliciting feedback ineptly, could permanently damage the relationship with his or her subordinates.

An alternative approach therefore would be to develop your own training programme. If fellow managers, not necessarily in the same organization, wish to improve their interpersonal skills, then they could get together informally to practise these skills and give each other feedback and guidance. The cases included in Chapter 2 could be used to provide the basis of role play exercises or these could be drawn from real life situations. Whilst this form of practice may not reflect the real life situation perfectly, it does have several advantages. The interaction can be recorded, thus providing an opportunity for more detailed and focussed analysis. The person role-playing the subordinate can be asked to play the role in the way which the manager would find most useful to practise on, e.g. aggrieved, angry, over compliant, taciturn, and so on. Furthermore, the manager can use the role play as an opportunity to try out questionning techniques, gambits, approaches, etc. which he or she would not normally use, without having to live with the results should everything not work out as planned.

This brings us to a final point. Should you decide to change the way you interact with subordinates on the basis of this book, we would recommend that you proceed by small steps. Firstly, this is because a sudden major change would surprise subordinates and give them problems in knowing how to handle it. Secondly, a major change may not produce exactly the results hoped for, and the unwanted repercussions could also be great. Minor changes, such as the use of more open questions or probes, using a somewhat more organized structure or departing somewhat from an over-rigid one, is unlikely to have a dramatic impact, adverse or beneficial. If the effect is beneficial, however, one can continue to experiment and expand the range of one's skills step by step.

REFERENCES

1   D Meister (1976), *Behavioural Foundations of Systems Development*, John Wiley.

2   CW Allinson (1977), 'Training in Performance Appraisal Interviewing: An Evaluation Study', *Journal of Management Studies*, Vol. 14, pp. 179–191.
    DS Taylor and PL Wright (1977), 'Training Auditors in Interviewing Skills', *Journal of European Industrial Training*, Vol. 1, pp. 8–10 & 16.

3   GA Randell (1982), 'Management Development Through Self-Analysis and Self-Tutoring'. Paper presented at 20th International Congress of Applied Psychology, Edinburgh.

APPENDIX I

MICHAEL'S PROSPECTS: SOME HYPOTHESES CONCERNING THE REASONS FOR INADEQUATE PERFORMANCE AND POSSIBLE SOLUTIONS

Possible Reasons For Performance Problem	Possible Solutions
Goal clarity Michael does not realize that his current performance and prospects will be evaluated as much in terms of his managerial effectiveness as his scientific merit	Let Michael know how importantly the company views managerial effectiveness (his section manager has made a start on this, but could have done so earlier)
Ability Michael has obvious scientific ability, but is poor at planning and is unable to schedule the total project effectively	Send him on a Critical Path Networking course
Task difficulty It may be too much to expect of a creative scientist to concentrate on both day-to-day management and the scientific pressures involved in innovation	Relieve Michael of responsibility for day-to-day management (NB, this is tantamount to admitting that he lacks management potential, and therefore other ways of providing status may have to be found)
Intrinsic motivation Michael finds challenge and excitement in scientific research, but little or none in management	Try to persuade Michael that there is also challenge and excitement in being successful at managerial activities
Extrinsic motivation Michael has received no rewards for managerial success from management or colleagues, but a great deal of admiration for his scientific achievements	Pay more attention to his managerial performance. Praise his successes. Draw attention to failures in a non-punitive way. Indicate that promotion prospects will be increased by improving managerial performance
Feedback Michael receives delayed or inadequate information concerning the consequences of his managerial actions	Provide immediate feedback
Resources Michael lacks planning aids which would help him to schedule his work. Alternatively, he needs secretarial/administrative assistance to take over routine work	Provide wall charts, secretary, personal assistant, as appropriate
Working conditions Although nothing is specifically indicated, it may be that Michael's office is merely a partitioned off corner of the lab, resulting in noise, interruptions, heat, fumes, etc.	Improve working conditions as appropriate

APPENDIX II

RECOGNIZING QUESTION AND STATEMENT TYPES

Answers to questions given on p. 73.

A Open
B Leading
C Reflective
D Multiple
E Summary
F Comparison
G Closed
H Probing
I Hypothetical
J Lubricator
K Bridge

APPROPRIATE USE OF QUESTION AND STATEMENT TYPES

Answers to questions given on pp. 73–74.

1 A Open
2 F Comparison
3 B Leading
4 I Hypothetical
5 C Reflective
6 K Bridge
7 J Lubricator
8 G Closed
9 E Summary
10 H Probing

APPENDIX III

DEALING WITH EMOTION AND FRUSTRATION

Answers to questions given on pp. 74–75.

1 (a) Poor response—inappropriate sympathy—closed questions irrelevant to frustration being expressed.

(b) Poor response—placating, excusing and inappropriate sympathy.

(c) Poor response—inappropriate sympathy, excusing or premature confrontation depending on tone of voice etc.

(d) Positive response which attempts to reflect back an understanding of the person's expressed feelings.

2 (a) Inappropriate reflective—judgemental in choice of word 'fault'.

(b) Poor response—judgemental/interpretive: it may be true but it has not been expressed.

(c) Good response—attempts to reflect back the stated problem.

(d) Poor response—either scathing or premature problem solving depending on tone of voice, etc.

3 (a) Good reflective insofar as it attempts to show understanding of the person's expressed feeling.

(b) Poor response—depending on how it is said could indicate lack of listening, premature confrontation or premature problem solving.

(c) Poor response—premature advice, rejection of complaint and no attempt to understand the frustration being expressed.

4 A positive statement should contain something like:
"You feel puzzled by his behaviour."
"You feel uncertain about how to behave with him."

5 A positive statement should contain something like:
"You seem to have got a lot of pleasure out of doing the job lately."
"You seem very satisfied with the job and have got a lot of pleasure out of it lately."

APPENDIX IV

A TRAINING COURSE FOR THE DEVELOPMENT OF THE INTERPERSONAL SKILLS OF LEADERSHIP

The precise content of the course would depend to some extent upon the needs of the managers and therefore the particular skills being developed. For example, there might be a need to develop skills for handling disciplinary or grievance interviews, fact finding, negotiations, day-to-day interaction with subordinates, and so on, and thus the emphasis of the course would change accordingly. For purpose of illustration, however, let us consider a course on performance improvement, because these can be designed to cover not only influencing behaviour but also gathering information and handling emotion.

Typically, courses using the 'Bradford Approach' to interpersonal skills training have 12 participants and last 2 days. The course outline is given in Figure 7, and follows closely the structure developed by Randell *et al.*[1] for training in performance appraisal interviewing.

Day One

Morning   PLENARY LECTURE/DISCUSSION (2½ hours)
The Interpersonal Skills of Leadership
- the role of the individual manager and the need for skill
- analyzing work performance
- observational skills
- performance skills

BRIEFING AND PREPARATION FOR ROLE PLAYED INTERACTIONS (45 minutes)

Afternoon   ROLE PLAYED INTERACTIONS (3 hours)
REVIEW OF ROLE PLAYS IN PLENARY (1¼ hours)
BRIEFING FOR SECOND DAY (15 minutes)

Day Two

Morning   PLENARY LECTURE/DISCUSSION
Handling motivation and emotion in manager–subordinate interactions (1½ hours)
BRIEFING AND PREPARATION FOR DAY TWO ROLE PLAYS (45 minutes)
ROLE PLAYED INTERACTIONS (1 hour)

Afternoon   ROLE PLAYED INTERACTION (2 hours)
REVIEW OF ROLE PLAYS IN PLENARY (1¼ hours)
COURSE REVIEW (open ended)

FIGURE 7 A Leadership Skills Development Course

The first morning is mainly taken up with a lecture/discussion session on the interpersonal skills of leadership. It briefly covers the material dealt with in Chapters 2–7 of this book. Its aim is to give a basic grounding in the need for and nature of the interpersonal skills of leadership.

This is followed by a short briefing session concerning the afternoon's role play exercises. The role plays are based on a performance improvement case of the type included in Chapter 2. For role playing purposes, however, the case has two sides—the same events as seen from the manager's viewpoint and that of the subordinate. The course members receive the manager's side of the case before coming on the course, and should be familiar with its contents. The aim of the briefing session is therefore to describe the format for the role plays, share ideas on how the case might be handled and clarify any points of detail. The subordinates are role-played by non-course members on the first day, often postgraduate students, but sometimes other members of the same organization as the course member's, if the course is run in-house.

In the afternoon, course members split into syndicate groups of three, each led by a tutor. Each member of the syndicate group then carries out one interview on the same case but with the subordinate role played by a different person. The format for each role play is as follows.

Role-Played Interaction (Approximately 30 minutes)
The 'subordinates' are briefed not to act the part, but to respond naturally to the manager as they would respond in real life if being treated in the same way. Thus, if the 'subordinate' is playing his or her role properly, the manager should receive his or her 'just deserts' in terms of the skill with which the subordinate is handled.

Analysis (Approximately 30 minutes)
The tutor then leads and participates in a discussion on the role-played interaction, eliciting the views of the manager who has just carried out the role play, the other two course members who observed it, and the person who role played the subordinate. By the end of this discussion, the manager should have a clear idea of:

- The effect of the interaction on the 'subordinate'
  - (a) emotionally—how the 'subordinate' felt at the end of the interaction
  - (b) behaviourally—what, if anything, the 'subordinate' intends to do differently in the way he or she carries out his or her job.
- What the manager did, or did not do, during the interaction which produced these results.
- What the manager is going to do differently next time, if faced with a similar situation, to produce even better results.

In the final session of the day, which is held in plenary, the head tutor asks each course member in turn what they achieved in their interaction, what they learned from it and, again, what precisely they are going to do differently in their next interaction to improve their performance. This is partly to check whether the learning points from the analysis sessions have been absorbed and to gain public commitment to them. More importantly, as Randell argues, it provides another opportunity to practise self analytic skills.

As shown in Figure 7, Day 2 begins with a more detailed discussion of motivation, and the Day 2 cases typically involve a heavier emphasis on motivational problems than Day 1. This reflects the complexity of the subject and, in our view, its importance in achieving performance improvements. However, this could be changed for course members with different priorities and other aspects of performance improvement could be emphasized on the second day. The remainder of the course repeats much the same format as the first day except that two different cases are used on Day 2 and the course members act as manager and subordinate in different role played interactions. This has two advantages. Firstly, it provides the 'manager' with feedback from a 'subordinate' who is by now familiar with the course contents and concepts. Secondly, it gives the 'subordinate' the opportunity to analyze what it feels like to be handled skilfully (or not, as the case may be) which may have important lessons concerning the way he or she handles his or her own staff.

This course represents a typical two-day course using the Bradford Approach to interpersonal skills training. However, the format can be modified to suit different purposes. If the main aim was to provide training for short day-to-day interactions between managers and subordinates, then shorter role plays would be used and the number of course members per syndicate group increased. Similarly, the course can be extended and the extra time used to set up practice sessions to suit the needs of individual course members. Some may wish to have another attempt at the standard type of case because they are not satisfied with their overall performance so far. Others may wish to practise particular types of interactions, such as grievance or disciplinary interviews and cases are available or can be improvised for this purpose.

REFERENCE

1   GA Randell, PMA Packard, RL Shaw and AJ Slater (1972), *Staff Appraisal*, Institute of Personnel Management.

APPENDIX V

A SELF DEVELOPMENT CHECKLIST

To be completed after a recent interaction with a subordinate.

1 **What were the objectives of the interaction?**
   (a) Handling Emotion
       — How did I want the subordinate to feel at the end of the interaction?

   (b) Gathering Information
       — What information did I wish to elicit?

   (c) Influencing Behaviour
       — What did I want the subordinate to do as a result of the interaction?

   (d) Other

2 **Outcomes of the interaction**
   (a) How did the subordinate appear to feel at the end of the interaction?

   (b) What new information did I have at the end of the interaction?

   (c) What actions have been agreed at the end of the interaction?
       (i) By the subordinate

       (ii) By me

   (d) What other outcomes were there?

3 **Did I achieve all my objectives?**
   (a) Yes—go to Q.4.
   (b) No—go to Q.5.

4 **Well done! Now, what can I do to maintain this level of performance or make it even better next time?**
   (a) Why was the interaction so successful?
       (i) Appropriate question and statement types?
           — If so, which did I use and why did they appear effective?

       (ii) Appropriate use of nonverbal cues?
            — If so, which did I use or observe the subordinate use and how did this affect the interaction?

       (iii) Appropriate structure?
             — If so, precisely how did I achieve the structure I used?

       (iv) Appropriate approach?
            — If so, what approach did I use and why was it appropriate?

(b) In what situations and with which subordinates would similar question and statement types, nonverbal cues, structure and approach also be likely to produce favourable outcomes?

(c) In what situations and with what subordinates would similar question and statement types, nonverbal cues, structure and approach be likely to produce *un*favourable results?

(d) Could anything be done to improve my performance, e.g. make it more elegant, achieve the same results in a shorter time?

Now go to 7.

5 In what way(s) were the outcomes of the interaction unsatisfactory? Give details under the appropriate heading(s).
  (a) Handling Emotion

  (b) Gathering Information

  (c) Influencing Behaviour

  (d) Other

6 In what ways did my handling of the interaction contribute to the unsatisfactory outcome(s)? Give details under the appropriate heading(s). If you are unsure why the interaction produced unsatisfactory outcomes, a number of hypotheses concerning the reasons why interactions may fail to achieve their objectives are suggested in Appendix VI.
  (a) Handling Emotion

  (b) Gathering Information

  (c) Influencing Behaviour

  (d) Other

7 Having analyzed the interaction, what could I do differently next time I am faced with a similar situation, in order to achieve a more successful outcome?
  (a) What should my main objective(s) be?
      (i) Handling emotions better

      (ii) Gaining more precise information

      (iii) Gaining commitment to a specific action plan

      (iv) Other

Specify as clearly as possible under each heading, where relevant, what you would like to achieve differently from the last interaction.

(b) In what ways would I like to carry out the interaction differently?
   (i) Verbal components used? If so, which?

   (ii) Nonverbal components used? If so, which?

   (iii) More effective or appropriate structure? If so, which?

   (iv) More appropriate approach to the interaction? If so, which?

APPENDIX VI

SOME HYPOTHESES CONCERNING REASONS WHY INTERACTIONS MAY PRODUCE UNSATISFACTORY OUTCOMES

(a) Handling Emotion

Objective: To reduce the subordinate's sense of grievance, frustration or anger.

Outcome: Subordinate still left with feeling of dissatisfaction.

Hypotheses:
- Insufficient use of reflectives, restatements, lubricators, apologies; over-use of closed and leading questions
- Inappropriate nonverbal cues, e.g. leaning back, lack of eye contact, fidgeting, etc.
- Insufficient attention to subordinate's nonverbal cues, e.g. signs of rejection, doubt, etc.
- Structure too rigid, insufficient listening or appearance of listening
- Inappropriate approach, e.g. Tell and Sell, attempting to solve the problem, rather than Ask and Listen until the subordinate has had a chance fully to express the emotion

Objective: To enhance the subordinate's sense of satisfaction, self esteem, sense of achievement.

Outcome: Subordinate seems dissatisfied, lacking in enthusiasm, responsiveness.

Hypotheses:
- Insufficient use of reflectives, restatements, lubricators whilst subordinate wishes to talk; insufficient praise; praise not well done, e.g. too general
- Structure too rigid, insufficient listening or appearance of listening
- Inappropriate approach for this particular individual

NB In both cases, the subordinate may wish both to express some emotion *and* to see some action as a result of the interaction, e.g. a grievance redressed or a reward for good performance. Usually, it is more effective to allow expression of the emotion first and then move on to action. However, if this is delayed too long, or not reached at all, then the subordinate may be dissatisfied because there have been no concrete outcomes from the interaction. If the subordinate's aspirations seem justified, therefore, then a move to problem solving or a discussion of rewards may be called for.

Objective: To make the subordinate aware that there are shortcomings in his/her performance about which he/she should be seriously concerned.

Outcome: The subordinate does not show concern, but is instead flippant, dismissive, angry or resentful.

Hypotheses:
- Lack of information gathering prior to or in the early stages of the interaction allowed the subordinate to produce mitigating circumstances to excuse his/her poor performance. An Ask and Tell approach using searching probes during the Ask phase might have produced the additional information which would have made the subsequent Tell—if still necessary—more relevant.
- Inappropriate technique during the interaction:
  - Lack of information *giving*. Subordinate not told the gravity of the situation. Adverse organizational and personal consequences of poor performance not spelled out precisely enough. Verbal and nonverbal

signals that situation is not really serious, e.g. "There's just one small matter we have to discuss" said with a smile and dismissive manner
— Diffusely structured interaction, allowed to go off main, serious topic into less tense side issues before the message is precisely stated
— Inappropriate approach, e.g. problem solving with a subordinate who comes up with unacceptable solutions. Try Tell and Sell if sure of facts, Ask and Tell if not.

(b) Gathering Information

Objective: To gather the information necessary to make a decision, either during the interaction or subsequently.

Outcome(s): ● The issue is left undecided during the interaction because insufficient information was gathered to make it with confidence, *or*
● A poor decision is made during the interaction because the information on which it was based was incomplete or erroneous, *or*
● The subsequent decision cannot be made because there is insufficient evidence to make it with confidence, *or*
● The subsequent decision is made, but turns out to be incorrect because it was based on erroneous information.

Hypotheses: ● Lack of information gathering components, e.g. open, probes, comparisons, particularly probes to follow up initial general information and nail down the precise fact(s) needed. Too many leading questions.
● Diffuse structures, wandering off the point before the precise information required is nailed down. No summary
● Inappropriate approach, i.e. anything other than Ask and Listen.

(c) Influencing Behaviour

Objective: To gain the subordinate's commitment to a plan of action which is intended to improve his/her performance.

Outcomes: Either (i) the subordinate is not committed to the plan or (ii) the plan is not as precise as you would like.

Hypotheses: (i) Subordinate not committed to plan.
● Lack of information gathering components. The plan does not seem workable to the subordinate or he/she thinks there is a better solution. More information gathering might have revealed the source of the subordinate's dissatisfaction or additional facts which would have enabled a better plan to be drawn up
● Over-use of criticism and under-use of praise of past performance, causing resentment on the part of the subordinate
● Lack of explanations of why the improvement in performance is organizationally desirable
● Lack of inducements to persuade the subordinate that the improvement is personally desirable. If the table on page 19 were filled in for this subordinate, would the benefits from good performance significantly outweigh the benefits from poor performance, and were the benefits from good performance spelled out in sufficient detail (promises and threats)?

NB 1. Threats are more likely to bring about compliance than commitment.

2. If insufficient is known about the inducements which would influence this subordinate, then information gathering on this subject may be called for.

- A diffuse structure, leading to no firm conclusions leaving the subordinate with the impression that the interaction was a 'non-event'.
- Inappropriate approach to the interaction, e.g. Tell and Sell with an experienced subordinate with useful ideas of his/her own, or Problem Solving with an inexperienced subordinate or one whose solutions are organizationally unacceptable.

(ii) Plan not sufficiently specific

- Insufficient use of information gathering components e.g. open questions and probes, to gather precise information needed, and summaries to crystallize solutions
- Diffuse structure leading to no firm conclusions or over-rigid structure preventing relevant information gathering
- Inappropriate approach to interaction (as above)

(d) Other

If none of above hypotheses apply in your case, the following questions may help you to pinpoint why the interaction produced less satisfactory outcomes than you would have liked.

(i) What verbal and nonverbal components did you tend to use most during the interaction?

Were there any components in particular which appeared to have an adverse effect on the subordinate's responses or the outcomes of the interaction?

(ii) How was the interaction structured?

Did this appear to have an adverse effect on the subordinate's responses or the outcomes of the interaction?

(iii) What approach did you use for the interaction?

Did the approach selected appear to have an adverse effect on the interaction?

Now return to Question 6, Appendix V.

Name Index

Subject Index